No Fuss
BABY &
TODDLER
Sleep

No Fuss
BABY &
TODDLER
Sleep

Niamh O'Reilly

MERCIER PRESS
IRISH PUBLISHER – IRISH STORY

MERCIER PRESS

Cork

www.mercierpress.ie

© Niamh O'Reilly, 2015

ISBN: 978 1 78117 317 6

10 9 8 7 6 5 4 3 2 1

A CIP record for this title is available from the British Library

Printed and bound in the EU.

CONTENTS

For Ava, Sive, Caoimhe, Andrew
and Jamie

I love you to the moon
and back

ACKNOWLEDGEMENTS

My mum has never really told us if she had to undertake any sort of sleep coaching with us as kids, but I'm pretty sure none of us were textbook children. So thanks, Mum, for doing everything you always did for us, while still allowing us to become well-adjusted individuals. Dad, thanks for at least pretending to understand my career choice! You have given the four of us a perfect start through your support and love (and the slipper placed threateningly outside your bedroom door at night – which, I might add, was never used).

My gorgeous nieces, Ava and Sive, have given me first-hand experience of what it is to love and adore two small people, while, at the same time, allowing me to practise what I preach!

I'm grateful for all the babies I have cared for over the years – not just in The Nursery, but all those I have helped along the way. Thank you so much to the parents – not only for the privilege, but also for your faith in the systems I helped to put in place for you all. You have been so kind in spreading the word and helping me reach so many others.

Aisling Wynne, thank you for helping me get my business up and running a few years ago. Anne Marie Dempsey and Suzanne McGloughlin, thank you. You both know why. And Leonie Henson, I can't begin to thank you for your wonderful, creative mind. The cover would not be what it is without your help.

A special thank you to Emily Rainsford Ryan and Christine Doran for their practical and helpful breastfeeding advice.

Finally, to all the team at Mercier Press and, in particular, Sarah Liddy, thank you for your support, patience and unwavering assistance along the way. Also, without the careful editing eyes of my aunt, Marie Dillon, and my lovely mum, Monica O'Reilly (who I realised, all too late, has a degree in English!), this publication may have been more of a leaflet than a book!

Names have been changed to protect the identity of all the families in my case studies. All parents gave me permission to include them, and I am so grateful to them all for doing so.

FOREWORD

LUCY KENNEDY

When my children, Jack and Holly, were having trouble sleeping during the night, or were waking up too early, we all struggled, and it was then that I turned to Niamh for professional advice. At the time, I was trying to be bright-eyed and bushy-tailed for the nation on 2FM's *Weekend Breakfast* show, but in reality I was often in a daze, with little or no recollection of the nights before!

Both I and my husband work, and were tired, emotional and at a loss. As busy parents, having a sense of what was going on with the kids, and needing them to play ball at least some of the time, was really important to us, in order to actually function in the world! Being so close to the situation, though, we were barely able to see the wood for the trees.

So, instead of questioning our own methods any further, we decided to trust someone who knew. That was Niamh.

Niamh gave us a simple routine to follow, which was easy to adopt and to understand. The routine also fitted in with our child-care situation at the time, so it wasn't too much of a change, particularly for Holly. Niamh showed us a simple plan for daytime, which really helped with the nights and those dreaded 4.30 a.m. starts. Best of all, it worked!

Niamh reassures you and keeps you motivated through the haze of exhaustion and diminishing will-power. Knowing that someone was on our side gave us the confidence to keep going, and to make the changes that ended up really suiting our family. Niamh in your life is a must-have when you have a baby or a toddler. Or, as in our case, both!

I really trust her advice and expertise.

Fan for life.

AUTHOR'S NOTE

Welcome to my baby and toddler sleep guide, where you will find tips and techniques to help you reach the Holy Grail – extended periods of uninterrupted sleep for your family. Here you will find ways to understand why little ones wake at night and why they need your support when nodding off. It is important to know just what causes sleep troubles and disruptions, and how to approach these challenges when you are already tired.

Firstly, some background information about me. I have always had a keen interest in and huge love of babies and children. I am the eldest of four children in a very close family and, as if that wasn't enough, I also have great relationships with my thirty cousins – who, in turn, have produced thirty-two babies, making up the next generation. They say 'It takes a village to raise a child', and that is certainly true in our case!

At the ripe old age of seventeen, back when I was leaving school, I really wanted to work somewhere in the field of childcare. Unfortunately (and in hindsight, misguidedly), my Career Guidance teacher had other aspirations for me; to keep everyone happy I enrolled in a Business Studies course. Nine years later I left my job in banking to study childcare full time. Finally, I was doing what I wanted. I have found my subsequent studies and work exceedingly rewarding.

After six years working in crèches, I fulfilled a long-held ambition and built my own nursery. For seven years, The Nursery became a little 'home from home' for babies aged from five months to eighteen months and a haven for (usually) first-time mums.

It was here that I was really able to see first-hand the difficulties parents were having in establishing good sleep habits for their children. Whilst in my care the babies would go down for their naps without much of a fuss, whereas at home anything could happen. For example, they might be allowed to fall asleep in the car or in buggies at all hours of the night. They might be sharing beds or simply sleeping really badly, no matter where.

My own favourite story (and the one that started me really thinking seriously about all of this) is of a set of parents who took turns to sleep on the floor of the baby's room, with one arm reaching into the cot – all night!

The parents and I had great relationships, and no child-related conversation topics were off-limits. I found myself advising them about sleep habits, using a combination of my training, my experiences in The Nursery, my gut feelings and my instincts. But I had a hunch that there was more to it. So I decided it was time to explore further the minefield of infant and childhood sleep.

I closed The Nursery as a childcare service and completed a Registered Sleep Coaching course in the UK. (I was awarded ninety-seven per cent, if you don't mind, and I assume the final three per cent was deducted for misspelling!)

So, for the past few years I have been busy consulting with families in their own homes and helping them to get their wide-awake babies into a more settled pattern of healthy sleep. I have worked with hundreds of families and it is no small boast that our track record has been excellent.

My scrapbook is filled with lovely messages of thanks received over the years from parents expressing appreciation for the help and support they received. They tell tales of relief and restorative calm in households where babies and children sleep soundly and regularly – and the parents do too!

It is easy to feel alone and upset if your child is not sleeping well and you find yourself walking the floors late at night. You can end up feeling that you are the only person in the world wide awake, in the middle of the night, suffering from sleep deprivation. Please be assured that this is not the case. You most definitely are not alone.

How to use this book

There is lots to choose from within these pages – handy daytime routines, simple explanations for various sleep disorders, tips for babies with reflux issues and simple but effective sleep techniques, to mention but a few things. You may wish to dip in and out and choose the sections that apply to you, rather than read the book from cover to cover.

If you are pregnant or have a very new baby and are hoping to get things on the right track from the beginning, start at chapter one for some advice about the early months. If your baby is more than six months old and still waking up a lot at night, chapter four, which looks at all the considerations around sleep training, will be useful.

Oh, and don't just go looking for the 'technique' straight away. I give you some background information at the start of the book, which is important as part of an overall approach to tackling sleep problems – you are less likely to give up if you understand the reasons why you're doing something!

And – before you ask – I am not a parent. Neither am I a parenting expert. I have never claimed to be one. But I have many, many years of experience with babies and toddlers and, by not having my own children I believe I can – more often than not – be a little detached from parents' situations in a helpful way. It allows me to take an overview of the 'big picture' in a family and to stand aside from the emotional side of things that can sometimes be overwhelming.

Lastly, healthy sleep outcomes are not all down to me. It is always you, the parents, who are the ones to put in the necessary hard work and commitment. However, I am pleased to tell you that it can be a surprisingly short-term investment, and one that brings change for the better. The outcomes can be life altering! There are no hard-and-fast rules, just your commitment and a promise to be consistent.

Reading and reflecting on the material in this book will do *nothing* in itself. Practice is key. I promise that the results will speak for themselves if you do invest your time and energy in making a commitment to change. Sleep will come.

Always keep in mind that my advice is just that: advice. I am here simply to help and offer practical reassurance and guidance. But, whatever you do, please, please, please be consistent. Confusion is the last thing your child needs in the wee small hours of the morning. As I constantly say to clients, 'Good luck. Be strong and be brave!'

I know about sleep.

Trust me!

1

PRE-BIRTH
AND NEWBORN
TO FOUR MONTHS

All grown-ups were once children ... but only few of them
remember it.

Antoine de Saint-Exupéry

As Julie Andrews sang in *The Sound of Music*, 'Let's start at the
very beginning ...' For all mums, but especially first-time mums,
having a baby means taking a step into the unknown, and it can be
daunting. Women now hold equal status in the workplace, where
their competence is recognised and rewarded. Then, seemingly in
the blink of an eye, a baby arrives and everything changes. Many
new mums find themselves questioning the smallest things: Is my
baby too warm? Too cold? Is it okay to let the baby sleep in the car
seat? Is that poo the wrong colour?

Nothing can adequately prepare new parents for the change
their new baby will bring to their lives. It can, paradoxically, be
both the most joyful and the most challenging of times. I have
often heard new mums saying they went from feeling confident
and independent to confused and lonely – in the space of just a

few hours! For some it is a smooth transition, but it is so hard to predict which course your journey will take. Many parents have told me that the greatest challenge following the birth of their first child was no longer feeling like they truly knew who they were. Life had changed so much for them that they felt frightened, with their very sense of self under threat. Questions like these arose: Am I me? Am I a wife? Am I a mother? Am I a lawyer/teacher etc.? How can I be all of these things – and yet still be *me*?

A new mother can sometimes feel lost in a fog. This feeling may be short-lived, or it can last for longer. Support is key at this stage, even if some women find it difficult to ask for help – or to accept it when it's offered.

Look after yourself

Even before your baby arrives, it is just so important to take time to be yourself and do those things that you love. Go for walks and enjoy meals out with your partner. Pre-baby date nights are to be cherished! I have recently heard of couples going on 'baby-moon' – a little holiday before their baby arrives. Obviously, not everyone can afford one of these, but it can be so beneficial to have that time as a couple looking forward to your new baby's arrival. Simply 'battening down the hatches' and spending a weekend at home together can also work, and keeps the costs down! Turn the phones off and just hang out; life is about to change, and seizing the opportunity to be alone together can help you to strengthen your ties and charge your batteries.

Be prepared

Once you have reached the later stages of pregnancy, you should be prepared for baby's imminent arrival. The baby may even come a wee bit early and catch you off guard! Have your hospital bag ready and waiting by the hall door. You may want to have two bags – a small one for the labour and your main one for after you have had the baby. Many hospitals will allow you to bring only your 'necessities' into the labour ward with you, so pack separately anything else you might need over your stay.

What do you need to put in this bag (or bags) waiting in the hall? Actually, not as much as you might think. Your partner might like a bit of breathing space outside the hospital, and going on errands for things you need could provide this, as well as giving you an opportunity to include him in meeting both mum's and baby's needs. There is a huge change going on in his life too!

Another reason to try to resist the temptation to pack too much if you will be staying on a hospital ward for a few days is that you may not have much storage space. Arrange for your partner or someone else to replenish the stocks you'll need while you are there. Below are some checklists to help with this. I've included a special list for mums having a scheduled Caesarean section (C-section), as in this case there can often be a little delay and some waiting around, depending on what is going on in the hospital on the day.

Checklist: labour bag for you

- Maternity notes with your birth plan, should you choose to have one.

- An old T-shirt or nightdress for labour, with front opening if you want to breastfeed straight away.

- An old pair of socks – who needs cold feet while in labour?

- Disposable/old knickers for after the birth.

- TENS machine (if desired).

- Small water spritzer for use during labour.

Checklist: main bag for you

- Spare nightdresses/pyjamas.

- Support bra/nursing bra, if breastfeeding.

- Dressing gown and slip-on slippers (to avoid having to bend down!).

- A couple of towels (large and small).

- Toiletries.

- Breast pads.

- Nappy bags – to get rid of nappies and your sanitary wear.

- Sanitary towel packs (maternity x 2).

- Any medication you are taking.

Checklist: C-section mums

If you know in advance that you are having a C-section, you'll probably have a little more time to think about what you'll need. You are also likely to have a longer stay in hospital, so factor this in when packing for yourself and the baby.

You may also find that you have a little more time on your hands in the hospital before the birth if you are having a section. Schedules may change and emergency situations may arise, which could put you at the end of the queue. Stockpile a few things to keep you occupied.

- Books and magazines.
- Music – CDs or downloads to your phone.
- iPad/tablet – don't forget your chargers for these!
- Once you have delivered your bundle of joy, the same things you need for a regular delivery will apply but bring high-waisted comfy knickers – you don't want any elastic waistbands sitting uncomfortably on your scar.

Checklist: hospital bag for baby

Double or, indeed, triple this if you have more than one baby coming!

- Long-sleeved babygros x 6+.
- Vests x 6+ (try to wash these before you pack them).
- Cardigan.
- Little hat.
- Pre-washed baby towel x 2.
- Pack of nappies (newborn).
- Cotton wool (not wipes).
- Bibs/muslin cloths.
- Baby blanket.
- Cot sheet.
- Car seat (ask someone to bring this in only on the day you are going home, as it will take up space and I am pretty sure the hospital won't let you store it).

Checklist: non-essentials (but nice to have)

Let dad/birthing partner take charge of this.

- Change for parking charges/payphone.

- Camera (although most people have great cameras on their phones so it mightn't be necessary).

- Light snacks, magazines, newspapers.

- Your own pillow (if you're allowed).

- Comfortable clothes for going home.

- Mobile phone charger.

- Eye mask (keeps bright lights in wards from interfering with your sleep).

- Earplugs.

- Arnica tablets (to help heal any bruising).

- A snack for dad – the last thing you need is a 'fainter' in the delivery room!

The new arrival and managing hospital visitors

You will be so excited and possibly a little overwhelmed when you meet your baby for the first time. You will want to show your little one off to the world with pride. But you may be exhausted! It is important to keep a close eye on your energy levels, as you will need all your resources to care for your precious new arrival – and yourself. I can't stress this enough. Try not to let too many people come in to see you while you are in hospital (in fact many hospitals allow only immediate family).

Use your stay as a valuable opportunity to rest and to learn about your little one and your new role in life. Ask for help, with anything at all, if you need it. No need or question is too little or too large! You will be with the experts, so take full advantage of their training and experience. The professionals are there to help and make your transition as seamless as possible. Take their advice – and my advice: just don't overdo things.

Coming home

The same advice applies when you get home. Well-meaning visitors may form a queue at your door. However, endless cups of tea and much admiration of your new baby can leave you feeling tired and emotional, particularly if you are also working to establish breastfeeding in the early days. Ask your friends to call ahead, rather than arrive on your doorstep unexpectedly. It can be hard to find a balance between having too many visitors and too few – but don't worry, you will soon learn how much space and alone-time you and your baby need!

It is important for you and your little one to have support and company when you need it, and also time on your own. Your partner can play a vital role in helping you to work this one out. Allow yourself the opportunity to choose a suitable time for visits. Friends and family will be looking forward to meeting your son or daughter, but for now, this time is about you, your new baby and your partner. Prioritising is important – you will never have those first few precious days back again.

Supplies

Stock up on freezer meals and washing powder ahead of time – be practical when it really counts. There's nothing worse than snuggling in for an afternoon at home and then realising that there's nothing appetising to eat! You have to do your best to eat healthily in order to keep your energy levels up. Accept all offers of food, especially cooked food, from well-wishers, and don't be afraid to ask people to pick up items for you. If a friend of mine has had a baby, I will send a text before going to visit her to see if she needs anything. Sometimes a good meal is valued more than a packet of vests or a cute outfit for junior!

On a practical note: believe me, there will be an awful lot of washing and laundry when your new baby arrives. Have plenty of non-bio washing powder at the ready. Even if you vastly overestimate the amount of washing you are going to do in the next few years, you still won't even come close to understanding how often you will fill that washing machine!

Sleep for you

You will have heard it before, but honestly, my advice is this: sleep when baby sleeps! It will do you the world of good.

You're not alone in thinking that your baby will stop breathing if you're not standing over the Moses basket looking in at all times. But you will do that child no favours if you become exhausted and strung out. A healthy mum is a happy mum! I know that this is not always possible, but at least try to make good use of the headspace or time out at your disposal when your little one naps. Do not use this time to engage in tiring activities – it is vitally important that you nourish yourself at each and every opportunity. These early days of infant care pass quickly, so make the most of your time and energy to ensure a rewarding experience.

Once baby arrives, make sure you don't neglect your partner. Dad and baby will benefit from spending time alone in these precious early days, and beyond. Remember, you can help to facilitate (or hinder) this!

In the early days, weeks and months of your baby's life, two issues are likely to preoccupy you most – feeding and sleeping. Both are basic needs, and your new baby may take a little time to settle into a pattern with them. However, approaching feeding and sleeping almost like a blank canvas will help you find your rhythm. Worry little about advice from friends and relatives until you establish your own pattern.

Preparing your home for a new arrival

Baby equipment and paraphernalia don't come cheap, and you may find you don't actually need everything you see recommended in magazines or online. Wait until you are setting up your baby's own room before going shopping. Holding off for a while will also give you a chance to save up for some of the bigger things you will really need. You definitely don't have to break the bank – at least for a while!

Where your baby will sleep

When it comes to sleep, there are a few things to consider. The leading health organisations recommend that babies sleep (particularly at night) in a cot beside their parents during the first six months of life. You probably won't want it any other way. Not only is this a good rule of thumb, but if you are planning on breast-feeding it simply makes most sense to have the little one near you. However, if you are setting up a baby's room from scratch, or simply making space for your baby in your own room, you have a few options as to where exactly your baby will sleep.

Moses basket

Initially, at night your baby will sleep (hopefully!) in a Moses basket beside your bed and during the day probably in the sitting room/kitchen, or wherever you spend your daytime hours. As a general rule, babies can stay in a Moses basket until they are about four months old, but for each baby the time varies depending on how big they become in that period. Most parents will choose to leave the base/frame in their bedroom and just transfer the top part of the cradle to other rooms during the day. I may be stating the obvious, but it is really very important to say this: *never* carry your Moses basket downstairs or around the house when your baby is in it. Once your baby is in there, the basket should remain stationary. Be sure always to place it on a hard, steady surface, well out of harm's way.

Co-sleeper

A 'co-sleeper' is a small cot that is open on one side. You can attach it to your bed, or pull it right up beside the bed as you sleep. This enables you to transfer your baby easily during the night for feeds. Once fed, you can place the baby back in their cot with little fuss. They are still beside you, but you won't be fearful of rolling onto them while you sleep. (This rarely, if ever, happens, by the way, but it is always a good idea to move baby back into the co-sleeper after a feed.) If you are using this co-sleeper type of bedding, then during the day your newborn can sleep happily in a pram elsewhere. Just make sure the mattress in the pram is a good one.

Cradle

A cradle has a lightweight frame and can usually be rocked from side to side. Many parents choose this as an alternative to a Moses basket, as they feel that the motion of rocking will help their little ones to fall asleep, which it does in many cases.

Do not worry that you are setting yourselves up for a lifetime of rocking by investing in one of these. If the rocking becomes a habit for your baby, this can be easily changed. Cradles are usually suitable for infants up to about six months old.

Cot or cot bed

Many parents will decide to have their infants sleep in a cot or cot bed from day one because they would like them to become used to the idea of being in their cot from the start. It can also dramatically reduce the expense of buying cradles or baskets for them. It is absolutely fine for a baby to sleep in a cot from birth from a safety point of view. But I think they look so tiny in there, and in my experience they will sleep more soundly in a more comfortable, cosy space. However, there is no harm in placing your baby in the Moses basket at night and into the cot for naps, if your aim is to get them used to the cot.

Mattress

I want to underline the importance of a good and safe mattress. A good-quality mattress is definitely an investment worth making. Your newborn will spend the vast majority of the first few weeks either in your arms or in a Moses basket, pram or cot, so don't scrimp when it comes to buying the mattress.

A sprung mattress is possibly your best option, as it will

maintain its shape for longer than other types, so you won't get that 'dipping' in the mattress as your baby gets bigger and starts to roll around in the cot. Sprung mattresses may be a little more expensive than others, but they are worth it in the longer term. If you go on to have a second child, or more, it is a bit of an unwritten rule that you buy a new mattress each time. This is not at all essential, but bear in mind that your baby's mattress should be clean and firm, and it should fit the cot correctly.

Make sure the level of the mattress base is set at the appropriate height for the baby. Once children start to pull themselves upright, or begin to stand up, then it is time to drop the base to a lower setting. This is really important if you decide to do any sleep coaching, as little ones may try to climb out if you are not reacting to them in the way they want or expect you to!

Sheets

Your cot sheets should ideally be 100 per cent cotton and should correctly fit your mattress. I suggest you buy them in bulk, as during your baby's first months you may find that not only do some nappies leak, but also your tiny, gorgeous 'bundle of joy' can release more fluid than you could imagine – from both ends!

Lighting

You might find that your little one will happily sleep 'any time, anywhere'. But right from the start, try to encourage good sleep habits by having baby sleep in a dimly lit room. If parents get into a good habit of keeping things dark – or at least a bit dark – then this encourages babies to start associating darkness with sleep.

Darkness also helps to produce melatonin, a sleep hormone.

Brightness will stimulate your little one and can also be a bit start-ling. Use side lamps where possible, rather than central lighting.

Blackout blinds, although not essential in your baby's first couple of months, are a good investment to make; once little ones can distinguish between day and night, the creation of darkness during the day will encourage solid blocks of sleep at naptime, along with the production of melatonin.

Mobiles

Music mobiles over the cot can be really useful for grabbing some time to jump into the shower, but when it comes to sleep I wouldn't recommend them. It can be handy to place your baby in the cot to watch the mobile rotate and thus provide stimulation, but the last thing you want at bedtime and naptime is a stimulated baby! So, I suggest that if you are thinking of buying a mobile, try to use it only for playtime or when you need to distract your baby for a while, not when sleep is your intention. There is a time and a place for both – but as your little one gets older, the time is probably not bedtime!

Monitors

There are plenty of different baby monitors available in baby stores – from the simple 'walkie-talkie' type to more elaborate systems that you can hook up to your TV. Choosing one can be a bit daunting.

In use, the simple monitors are often just as good as the high-end ones – with one exception. Several brands have an added feature: a sensor mat which you place in the cot where your baby will lie. These monitors will detect sounds in the same way that a regular monitor will, but they will also notify you when there is no movement after a certain period of time. They can provide real peace of mind for parents. The only downside is that if you go to feed your baby during the night, once you lift the little one you have only a few seconds to turn the sensor off or it will start beeping away and the whole house could be awake! But, more often than not, turning it off will become second nature after a few false starts.

White noise

A variety of musical sounds and soothing noises can also be helpful when you are encouraging sleeptime for your baby. Many people swear by the sound of the hairdryer, or various white noise sounds in the background – you can buy these on CD or download them as apps. While initially they are useful, they can quite often become a crutch; your little one can become dependent on them very quickly in order to fall asleep. I suggest that you use these gadgets while you are winding down and settling your baby, but that you turn them off just as the little one is about to fall asleep.

White noise and other sounds are sleep aids. I will talk later on about such aids, and also about sleep associations and the differences between them (see chapter 3, pp. 89–91).

Room temperature

The recommended temperature for a baby's room is somewhere between sixteen and twenty degrees Celsius. Three bodies in a bedroom can have an impact on this, so be mindful of temperature fluctuations overnight, particularly if they are sharing a room with you.

Don't get too hung up on exact figures here. If you are warm, you can be pretty sure your baby is feeling this temperature increase too. The opposite also applies: obviously, if you are feeling chilly, so will your little one. Babies can't self-regulate their body temperature until they are approximately six months old, so it is your responsibility to monitor this as best you can.

Some handy baby monitors which show room temperature are available, and they can be quite useful if you are inclined to worry about this. But, like anything electronic or 'gadgety', you would be as well off going with your own instincts on how warm or cold you are feeling. Trust yourself. Have a little cardigan handy for baby, or be prepared to remove any extra blankets, just in case.

Clothing and swaddles
Baby sleeping bags

Gro-bags are handy for night-time, but not necessarily for a new-born. They are simply too small to fit into them properly, and a few cellular (breathable) blankets work well at this stage instead. These are easy to recognise as they have the little holes in them. They are available in every baby store.

Swaddling is another great way to encourage comfortable sleeping for your little one – but I will say more on this subject later on (see p. 33).

Seasonal changes

Although I do feel that our summers are getting a bit warmer, Irish weather is, for the most part, pretty predictable. We do not live in a country of massive weather extremes, and temperature changes are mostly gradual.

Winter

Have a cosy bedroom for night-times, rather than using blankets excessively. There will be times when you will need blankets, though, so invest in some cellular (breathable) blankets.

Some people like to warm up the Moses basket or cot before bedtime with a hot-water bottle. If you do this, remember to remove it once your baby goes down to bed.

Many people will also keep their little one's feet warm by using socks over the babygro, even though their feet are already covered. Little hands are often exposed while babies sleep, so putting a pair of socks on their hands may help to keep them warm. This can be quite effective for young babies, as they have a terrible habit of scratching their gorgeous faces while they sleep. However, if your baby uses a soother, I would advise not bothering with 'hand socks' when they are older, as you want them eventually to be able to try to put the soother back in their mouths themselves. (That's a bit tough if they can't wriggle their fingers!)

Summer

Once the temperatures outside start to rise, it is perfectly okay to have babies sleep in their vests, nappies and a light sleeping bag. At this time, make sure that your baby is drinking enough water during the day to prevent dehydration.

It is also okay to have the window open in summer. During the day, when baby is not sleeping, leave the window open, but perhaps pull the blinds or curtains so that the sun doesn't heat up the room too much.

No matter what time of the year it is, though, airflow in the cot and in the room is important. Remove bumpers and extra 'stuff' from the cot to enable the air to get around freely.

Once your child moves into a bed, keep pillows and soft toys to a minimum. Older children may also need a sippy cup of water beside the bed to keep them hydrated during the night.

Swaddling

Something I often recommend for babies – even up to about ten to twelve weeks – is swaddling. Swaddling can be very helpful in providing a blissful feeling for baby. The feeling is akin to being back in the womb, or being held in an embrace. It feels good and is familiar. However, don't immediately accept a child's seeming not to want to be swaddled. You may find that over time they really like it. So I suggest that you make an effort to at least try. It's about practice and persistence, with the aim of getting it right for both of you.

To swaddle your baby effectively, good-quality blankets are important. They don't have to be specific 'swaddling blankets', but the fabric does need to be pretty stretchy and, most importantly, breathable.

A 'too-tight swaddle' can lead to overheating and breathing issues, so please take care. Babies move around – even the littlest ones – and you may find that they can do a 'Houdini' out of their swaddles. So, should the blanket rise above the baby's face during a nap or sleep, the fabric type will be crucial. Cellular blankets are ideal for this purpose.

Note: Once your little one is able to roll onto his or her tummy whilst asleep, you should stop swaddling, as there could be a risk of suffocation. In fact, once you see even the potential for rolling you should consider stopping.

Another thing to take into account is some research by Professor Nicholas Clarke, a consultant orthopaedic surgeon at

Southampton General Hospital. His research revealed that the practice of tightly swaddling a baby (particularly if you straighten the baby's legs and wrap securely around the lower limbs) could increase the chances of the baby's developing hip dysplasia. Babies' hip ligaments relax during the birthing process, and if you force them to be in a particular swaddled position too often in the first few months, their hip joints may have difficulty strengthening and the muscles aren't free to move. I spoke to an orthopaedic surgeon whilst writing this book, and he mentioned that Inuit mums would generally swaddle their infants and they have the highest known instances of hip dysplasia. It isn't known whether that is as a result of swaddling too tightly, or maybe a genetic issue.

I am not trying to strike fear into you, so just use your common sense. If it seems too tight, it probably is. So, to this end, I suggest swaddling quite tightly or cosily around the baby's upper body but leaving the lower limbs a little bit freer to move.

Swaddling – step by step
Step one
Take a large, breathable, rectangular baby blanket and lay out on a flat surface. Fold one corner towards the middle of the blanket. Place baby's head along the edge of the folded area. With one hand on your baby, holding one of their arms down along their body, wrap a corner piece of blanket around your baby and tuck it in under the baby's bum (see Figure 1).

Step two
Next, fold the bottom part of the blanket upwards, although not so tightly as to restrict relatively free movement of legs, feet and

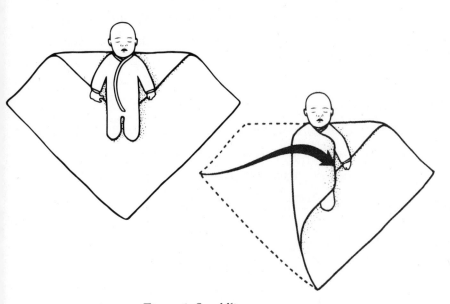

Figure 1. Swaddling: step one.

Figure 2. Swaddling: step two.

hips (see Figure 2). You may choose not to tuck up this 'bottom' part, but it's a personal choice. (As always, follow safe guidelines as recommended.)

Step three

Holding that last fold in place, take your final corner and wrap it around your baby, again tucking it in at the back (see Figure 3). Make sure that there are no uncomfortable lumps underneath when baby lies down.

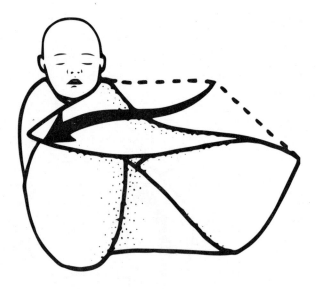

Figure 3. Swaddling: step three.

Step four

Tuck in any loose corners to provide comfort and security. Only the baby's head, neck and the top of the shoulders should be out of the swaddle (see Figure 4).

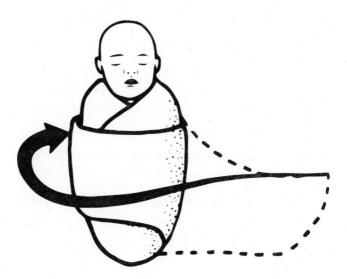

Figure 4. Swaddling: step four.

Changing recommendations about swaddling

One of my clients told me that one of the current swaddling recommendations in the maternity hospital she attended suggested a 'one-arm swaddle'. In this type of swaddle, you would leave one of your baby's arms free. I have to say, though, this is not something I have come across very often in my practice.

As with many things, health service recommendations change quite often, so talk to your GP or public health nurse if you are unsure about whether or not to swaddle. Swaddling is used widely in hospitals, where there are always midwives and staff in the rooms. My sister – a midwife – has said to me that a swaddled child should not be left unattended. Her advice is worth considering, although most newborns are rarely very far from one or other parent at any given time.

Sleeping arrangements for multiples

A number of years ago, a study was carried out at Durham University, researching the sleeping arrangements (not the sleep habits) of twin babies. Of the sixty sets of twins participating in the study, sixty per cent were co-bedding (sharing a cot) at one month of age. One-third of these babies were in individual cots by month three. It is unclear whether they were still in their parents' room or not at this age.

Interestingly, though, a higher proportion of parents of twins than parents of single babies had 'evicted' their babies and placed them in their own rooms three months earlier than parents of single babies.

A number of options are available when newborn twins or multiples come home for the first time. Depending on the hospital policy, the siblings may have shared a cot right from the beginning. Many premature twins, however, will have spent a little time away from each other during the first days or weeks of life. It is a personal choice, but bear in mind the National Institute for Health and Care Excellence (NICE) guidelines for safe infant sleeping, which recommends that there be sufficient airflow around the babies when they sleep and that they should be placed on their backs to sleep, in order to minimise the risks of SIDS.[1]

Co-bedding

Co-bedding refers to twins or multiples sharing a bed with each other. With co-bedding, the babies sleep together in the same cot.

---

1   Draft Recommendations to Tackle Sudden Infant Death Syndrome published for consultation, July 2014.

From early on they will enjoy great comfort from each other by sleeping in this way, and are often calmer when their sibling(s) is beside them. This mode of sleeping is unlikely to last too long, though. Once your twins or triplets are able to move around a little, they may disturb or startle each other during the night, and this may put an end to the practical advantages of cot sharing.

If your cot is big enough, one way of positioning twins to keep them together for just a little longer would be to place both babies in the cot, with their heads in the middle of the cot and their feet pointing towards opposite ends of it.

But, in general, from around six months of age, most twin babies will sleep better while occupying their own sleep space. Twins should not share small cribs or Moses baskets, as they may overheat in such a limited space. So, should you want them to sleep together, buy an extra-large cot for them to share.

Co-sleeping

I believe co-sleeping will appeal more to breastfeeding mums than to those who have decided to bottle feed. I usually suggest to mums of twin babies that they consider buying a co-sleeper to have beside their bed (as I described earlier under the 'Co-sleeper' heading on p. 26). One baby will lie beside you and one in the co-sleeper.

I think this is likely to be the easiest way of simply swapping their places over while you feed them during the night. Remember, once again, to follow safe sleeping guidelines.

Separate cots/Moses baskets, in a different room from parents from day one

Quite often, multiples (and in particular triplets) never sleep in their parents' bedroom. Rather, they are in a room with a bed for whoever happens to be 'on duty' that night. This could be mum or dad, perhaps even another family member, or a maternity nurse if the family can afford that luxury! Most parents of twins or multiples will be able to avail themselves of some form of help.

So, where with the single babies I talk about moving them out of your room, in the case of twins and multiples it is more likely that it will be a gradual withdrawal of your presence as time goes by. That is, you will be leaving their room rather than them leaving yours!

A separate room for each baby

This is the least likely of all the arrangements. Most parents will not feel that it is fair or wise to separate their twin or multiple children. And they will be right. Your babies genuinely will get great comfort from each other and will be pretty unlikely to wake each other much at night. However, if there is a sleep problem, then it is a different story.

Twins, multiples and, to a lesser extent, siblings are rarely bothered by each other's crying. The chance that their crying will wake another child in the family is a source of greater concern for parents. But if one twin does seem to wake the other, and they are still sharing a cot, then it might be a good idea to separate them at this point – providing one cot each for naps and bedtime. In this case, if you have the extra bedroom, I would even suggest you place them in different bedrooms, particularly if persistent waking at night is going on, and for the purposes of training. Some people will prefer not to separate them in different rooms, and I can understand the hesitancy. But for the sake of sleep, it might be a better short-term option. You can always move them back together again once you have resolved any sleep issues.

Sudden Infant Death Syndrome (SIDS)

None of us ever wants to talk about a baby dying, but it is important that we are aware of the guidelines around this issue. Sudden infant death syndrome (SIDS) 'is the unexplained death, usually during sleep, of a seemingly healthy baby less than a year old. SIDS is sometimes known as crib death because the infants often die in their cribs'.[2]

SIDS is not the same thing as a 'sleep-related accident', such as accidental smothering or suffocation, even though incidents of this type are extremely rare.

No reasons are known as to why SIDS occurs, although there are some known risk factors. To reduce any risks, please be sure to follow these guidelines:

- No smoking around infants – keep their environment smoke free at all times.

- Place infants on their back when going to sleep. As they grow and start to move a little, keep an eye on them that they haven't rolled over, particularly if they are being swaddled.

- Place their feet towards the foot of the cot.

- Limit the use of loose blankets as these can become a hazard and be moved around as children sleep.

2   Mayo Clinic (USA), http://www.mayoclinic.org/diseases-conditions/sudden-infant-death-syndrome/basics/definition/con-20020269, 17 May 2014.

- Keep room temperature between sixteen and twenty degrees Celsius.

- Make sure there is adequate airflow not only in the room, but also in the cot. To ensure this, there should be no toys or bumpers in or around the cot.

- Use a soother to help your baby fall asleep. Despite what you may have thought, NICE recommends soothers for babies up to one year of age.

- Share the bedroom with your child for up to six months.

- NICE recommends that you avoid co-sleeping and bed-sharing (where baby stays physically in your bed for the night and makes very little use of the cot). But the reality is that many new parents do choose these options (particularly if they are breastfeeding). If this is the case in your home:

  ○ Make sure that you or your partner are not overtired and that you haven't been drinking or taking drugs or medication.

  ○ Ensure that your bed is absolutely safe for your baby, with a flat, firm mattress and no gaps between the mattress and headboard.

  ○ Remove all pillows and bedding (duvets and blankets) in the early months, and dress both baby and yourselves warmly to compensate.

  ○ If you are breastfeeding and are concerned about 'falling asleep on the job', try getting out of bed to feed in an armchair. (Many breastfeeding mums find themselves unintentionally bed-sharing if they fall asleep while feeding.)

Remember, particularly in relation to co-sleeping and bed-sharing, these are the guidelines and recommendations from NICE, and I do not want to come across as contradicting myself when I talk about these issues. What I will say, though, is that both co-sleeping and bed-sharing, once undertaken safely and managed well, may indeed be the right choice for your family. As a sleep coach, I feel that babies and parents are not always getting quality sleep as a result of bed-sharing, but I am aware that it is the choice of many. I would suggest that once your baby is no longer feeding at night, this would be the time to make a permanent move to the cot.

Safe sleeping in cot/Moses basket/pram

Another term that some use for SIDS is 'cot death', but it is important to remember that SIDS may not necessarily occur in the cot. It can happen at any stage, even in car seats or, in fact, right beside you or in your arms. For more information on SIDS see the 'Useful contact details' on p. 223.

Car seat safety

Avoid the chances of little ones overheating when they are strapped in their seats. So, in cold weather, rather than a heavy snowsuit, use a lighter jacket and hat and tuck a blanket in around them to keep them warm. In fact, I have recently seen special car seat covers that reduce the need even for blankets. These cover the entirety of the seat, draping over your baby, but leaving his or her little face uncovered. They keep wind and rain away from your comfy baby when getting in and out of the car!

Avoid having too many blankets or cuddly toys round them in the car seat. These can add to the risk of suffocation.

A little science: types of sleep

We need not get too bogged down in the science of sleep. But it is worth noting that there are broadly two types of sleep: REM and non-REM.

REM stands for 'rapid eye movement', and this type of sleep is the more 'active' part of sleep, which both adults and children experience. During REM sleep your mind is still 'busy' in a way, but your body is, in a sense, paralysed. We are more likely to dream during this phase of sleep.

Non-REM sleep is different in that it is quite a deep sleep. Throughout the night we all pass between these two phases fairly regularly, but infants experience this deep sleep phase at the beginning of the night, and again quite early in the morning.

As babies get older, their sleep becomes more adult-like. They start to sleep in more separate bursts of each phase. For example, while your newborn will go in and out of sleep for most of a twenty-four-hour period, your six-month-old may start to show you that he or she can sleep for longer periods in the early part of the night. For example, six-month-olds may manage to go from 7 p.m. to 11 p.m. without waking. This is because their sleep pattern is changing, and they spend more time in that deep, zonked-out sleep. After these first few hours, they will go in and out of that heavy sleep, but it will not be as deep as it is in the first part of the night. As they move between these phases, they can be more likely to become disturbed as the change takes place. This is normal!

It's okay not to have a sleep schedule or routine with your brand-new baby; up to about six months of age it is certainly not crucial. Patterns will start to emerge all by themselves for most babies. Find your 'normal' and work around it. Of course your baby is a human child, not a robot – he or she won't come programmed to fit into your life. In the early stages the adjustment will be on the side of the mature adult accommodating the needs of the baby.

Sleep deprivation

Lack of sleep for adults is torturous. For little ones it's equally hard. Establishing a good sleep regime for everyone is just so important. Most adults require eight hours' sleep a night to function at their best. (Unless you are like Margaret Thatcher, who famously said, 'Sleep is for wimps!' and claimed she got by on four hours' sleep a night.)

There is evidence to show that broken sleep is almost as bad and as harmful to your well-being as no sleep at all. A recent study from a university in Tel Aviv found that parents who were sleeping seven hours a night, yet experienced broken sleep during this time, felt only the effects of half that amount of sleep. Waking up throughout the night with your little ones can, over time, give rise to exhaustion, and this can sometimes have serious consequences.

Recently there was a TV series called *Bedtime Live* on Channel 4 about children and sleep. One episode focused on the effects of sleep deprivation amongst parents of babies and small children. It featured a simulated driving experiment and included participants who had been regularly woken at night by their children. Other volunteers were given a number of alcoholic drinks before getting into the simulated car. The experiment revealed that a tired mum was more at risk of crashing, or falling asleep at the wheel, than those who had taken the drinks. Is it not frightening to think of so many people trying to function on a daily basis on little or no sleep?

AGE	DAYTIME SLEEP (HOURS)	NIGHT-TIME SLEEP (HOURS)
NEWBORN (UP TO 3 MONTHS)	Up to 19/20 hours between day and night	
INFANTS (FROM 3–6 MONTHS)	4 hours	11–12 hours
INFANTS 6–12 MONTHS	Up to 3 hours	11–12 hours
TODDLERS (12 MONTHS–2.5 YEARS)	2 hours	11–12 hours
PRE-SCHOOL CHILDREN (UP TO 5 YEARS)		11–13 hours
SCHOOL-AGE CHILDREN (5 YEARS +)		10–12 hours

Figure 5: Table showing the total number of hours of sleep required at different ages, and how this sleep is split between night and day.

Sleep deprivation in grown-ups gives rise to poor judgement, low or fluctuating mood, poor decision-making, physical exhaustion, confusion, depression, fatigue, poor attention span – the list goes on. Of course, it is completely normal to be tired in the first few weeks and months of your baby's life. But if you are still not getting sufficient sleep after several months have passed, it might be time to take action.

What to expect from newborn sleep

It is perfectly normal for your newborn to sleep for most of the day and most of the night, only really rousing for feeds or nappy changes. It is also quite normal to find that your baby may be a little more difficult in the evenings. Certainly for the first six to eight weeks this might be the case, and there is little you can – or, in my opinion, should – do to change this. That's not to say there won't be babies who will sleep really well at night from the moment they are born.

Newborn babies wake, for the most part, because they are hungry. It is that simple. So when they wake they must be fed. Please don't deny feeds to your newborn baby because you want them to stretch out the intervals between feeds so they will sleep longer. It is unfair to the baby, and I believe it is even a little cruel to do so.

You may have gathered by now that I do not recommend any strict schedules with your newborn. But that is not to say that you can't begin to encourage a few good habits right from the start.

Let your newborn sleep wherever he or she likes during the day – even if it is in your arms for the first while. Use a baby carrier too. It is important that you are physically close to your baby. Babies love this closeness and it makes them feel secure. These little ones need to be getting adequate sleep in the first few months – a rested baby is a happy baby. Don't be worried that you are creating bad habits. We can resolve them if they really become a problem. The priority here is the sleep, not the location!

Having said that, encouraging or allowing babies to 'rest' a while in their cot or basket will help them to realise that it is not a scary place to be – instead they will begin to discover the safety and security in their new world. When your little one is calm, lay him or her down for a rest, even when you don't think baby will actually sleep. Resting in itself is good – for all of us!

When your newborn is awake during the day, keep things bright. While the little one is sleeping, dim the lights or close the curtains. Let your baby's body clock naturally adjust to day and night by using curtains and natural daylight to your advantage.

Fresh air is a great way to encourage sleep. Get yourself and your baby out for walks if you can during the day. If you are post C-section and still struggling to get back on your feet, ask someone to bring your little one out for a stroll. Even thirty minutes will be a great help and it will give you a chance to have a quick nap too, so everyone wins! Even as little ones get older, and you are trying to get yourselves into a routine, I would encourage you to go out in the afternoons and take in some fresh air – get out to the park or simply go for a walk. If babies catch a nap in a buggy at that later part of the day, it may encourage them to sleep better at night. They won't be overtired going to bed and therefore will be less likely to struggle to get to sleep in the first place. There is a fine line between being tired enough and being overtired.

Baby massage is also a lovely way to keep your baby calm. Baby-massage classes are popping up all over the place. Whilst they are great, and can be a nice social gathering for new mums, you may prefer to find a few ideas online and practise yourself at home. It is a great way of bonding with your new baby.

When to start a routine

Many people ask about settling their newborns and getting them into a routine, but I just don't agree with pushing this on a new baby. I suggest you try to take at least the first twelve to fourteen weeks to get to know your baby, and for the baby to get to know you. Some babies will find their rhythm a bit more quickly, but don't worry about it too much if they don't. In my opinion, it is a little unfair, and not very wise, to put pressure on yourself, never mind on your tiny infant, so early on.

So, for brand-new parents, I say relaxing is the priority. Try to enjoy your early days and weeks together. They go by very fast. You will get to know your baby and you will definitely not be doing anything 'wrong' by going with the flow a little.

Feeding

Breastfeeding

Newborn babies will breastfeed *at least* every two to three hours, around the clock. So, in a twenty-four-hour period, they may feed as many as twelve times! They are not only feeding for themselves, but in the first few days they are also helping you to establish your milk. So, this is a win-win for everyone. I would also recommend that you should not expect a breastfed newborn to go more than three hours without a feed, even at night.

By six to eight weeks of age the number of feeds in a twenty-four-hour period will likely have reduced to approximately seven to eight feeds.

Feed your baby on demand if needs be, or if you enjoy doing it this way. They need what they need. So let them take as much as they want, when they want it.

Bottle feeding

If you are bottle feeding, I would suggest offering 2–3 fluid ounces (60–90 millilitres) per feed. They may or may not take it all though. Don't ever force-feed your baby. Feeding in tune with your baby's needs is the key to a good feeding experience and a good relationship. Don't insist that your baby drinks a certain amount just because the formula box tells you so!

The idea of never waking a sleeping baby doesn't work for me, particularly in the case of the teeny-tinies. Most new babies will lose some weight in the first few weeks, so it is important to feed them as often as your paediatrician recommends until they at least gain that weight back. Lift newborns, even if they are sleepy, if they haven't fed for three to four hours – you don't necessarily have to wake them fully, but you can offer a feed anyway. Often, something is better than nothing.

From around six to eight weeks babies will start being able to manage greater quantities at each feed, usually 3–4 fluid ounces (90–120 millilitres) per feed. You may be able to increase both the feeds and the length of time between feeds. They will soon be able to start 'stretching out' the intervals between feeds. Once they get to about sixteen weeks you can feel more relaxed and leave them to sleep for longer periods at night.

Winding

Young infants should be winded after each feed. Even if they seem to get wind up quite easily, I would always spend an extra few minutes winding them to see if they have any more hidden in there! If it seems to be taking a while, change your positioning – this simple adjustment may encourage your little one to burp. If babies go down to sleep and have not been winded properly, particularly in the early months, it can lead to them experiencing pain and, therefore, interrupted sleep.

You also don't have to wait until the end of a feed in order to burp your infant. Newborns will not be able to take much milk without needing to take a break for wind, so be aware that they may need to be winded after every ounce or two. If they are fussing while feeding, they may be in discomfort. In this case stop, have a break, and use this as an opportunity to get some air released!

There are many techniques for winding. It is a matter of finding one that suits you and is comfortable too (for you and baby).

One option is to place your baby in your arms and let the little one's chin rest on your shoulder. This is generally very comfortable for you and it allows you to firmly support the baby's head and neck.

Another option is to lie your baby across your knee so as to place a slight pressure on his or her tummy. This is not suitable for a baby who regularly spits up, as the extra pressure may cause the little one to vomit more than usual. Whilst your baby is across your knees, you can rub or gently pat him or her on the back to encourage baby to get the wind up.

My preferred method is to have the baby sitting upright on your knee and with you placing one hand under baby's chin (so that the head rests between your thumb and forefinger). It is a good position for your baby as he or she is upright. Rub or pat your baby gently on the back with your other hand. This 'hold' also allows you to gently rock the baby forward and back in order to encourage production of some wind.

Whichever option you choose, have a muslin cloth nearby (or already in place on your shoulder or knees) to catch any spit-up that may come your way!

Colic and reflux

I'm desperately trying to avoid talking about the bad stuff, particularly for readers whose babies have yet to arrive, but this is really worth mentioning. The incidence of children presenting with reflux is on the rise. I have seen it in my own practice over the last few years. Whether it is because of cases going undiagnosed in the past, or maybe even environmental factors, I am not sure, but I have found that at least forty per cent of my clients have mentioned that reflux (both mild and severe cases) had been an issue for a period with their babies.

'Colic' and 'reflux' are terms that are often used to describe crying and restless babies in the early months, but they are quite different in reality. Although neither colic nor mild reflux may need medical intervention, severe reflux will require medication and it is worth visiting your GP or paediatrician if you are worried, to have your little one diagnosed for sure.

Colic

Colicky babies are known to find it difficult to settle in the evening. Their day can go well, but from late afternoon to late at night they can be difficult to settle and may cry – sometimes a lot. Quite often it is a different cry to any others you may hear during the day. They almost scream, will more often than not raise their legs in towards their tummy and can be pretty inconsolable. I have heard this problem described by a paediatrician as 'crying for longer than three hours per day for at least three days a week'.

For parents, it seems as though nothing you try has any lasting effect. Colicky babies may settle for a moment with rocking, feeding or a soother, but the reprieve can be short-lived and then they set off screaming again. This can last for several hours – even up to five hours – but it will only happen once in the day and generally at the same time. Unfortunately it mostly happens in the evening – when parents are already exhausted and would do anything to 'make it stop'.

If your baby is simply fussy in the evenings and is just 'giving out', then the reason is not likely to be colic. In fact the chances are that your little one is just overtired and is finding it hard to settle down after the day. Should any persistent crying be accompanied by a fever, it is always advisable to seek medical attention immediately.

The bad news is that there is really no quick fix for colic. But the good news – as is the case with many other baby issues – is that this too will pass! Generally, by around twelve weeks of age most babies will have outgrown these episodes. Although no real explanations for colic are available, it is generally thought that wind or indigestion could be the cause of the pain.

There is no evidence to show that formula-fed babies or breastfed babies are more likely to be colicky. And, honestly, my own enquiry into this with a number of medical personnel has also revealed that nobody really knows definitively why it happens. Still, there are some things that may help you manage things until the stage passes:

- Swaddling can help a lot, so wrap your baby's upper body tightly enough but not too tightly. (See the swaddling guidelines on pp. 33–37.)

- Feed your baby in an upright position where possible to reduce any chances of taking in air when feeding. Also, check that your baby is not struggling to feed through a slow-flow teat. If babies have to work too hard while sucking, they may take in more air whilst feeding.

- Simply hold your little one when he or she experiences a bout of colic. Putting baby down continually may exacerbate the problem. Try a rocking chair in a calm room with low lighting.

- Do *not* repeatedly change the type of formula you are using. It is too much for a baby's little tummy to cope with. If you genuinely feel it is a digestive issue, and the crying is more prevalent around feeding times, then it is unlikely to be colic. It may be reflux or lactose intolerance. Seek medical advice.

- Use a soother. The sucking motion can serve to distract your baby a little.

- If you are breastfeeding, avoid spicy foods and caffeinated drinks, including tea and coffee. (Although I can appreciate that you may feel you need the caffeine simply to keep your energy levels up!)

- Use the buggy in the evenings, or a sling, as motion can help.

- Look for and take support when it is offered. Dealing with a crying baby can put a parent under a lot of pressure, and it's tiring, too!

- Remember the act of crying itself will not cause your baby any harm.

There are some over-the-counter medications available from your pharmacist. Don't buy them haphazardly but instead talk to your GP before giving any medication to your child. Just because it is on the shelves in a pharmacy does not mean it is the right thing for your baby.

Reflux
Reflux can present in a number of forms. The first and most obvi-

ous is a baby who vomits and spews up regularly after feeds – and in many cases, in between feed times too. With reflux, the 'vomit' has a quite distinctive acidic smell, and baby will cry, seemingly relentlessly.

There is also a silent form of reflux. In this case the baby will not normally be physically sick, but will scream in pain during and around feeds. This can be harder to diagnose as there is no 'physical sign' apart from the tears.

When acid from the tummy leaks upwards (the wrong way) into the gullet (oesophagus), the condition is known as acid reflux. Acid reflux is very common, particularly in young infants. Not all forms will require medical intervention. In fact the majority of young infants have some degree of reflux. This causes no problem and resolves spontaneously with time.

However, some infants have more severe forms of reflux – referred to as gastro-oesophageal reflux disease (GERD), including oesophagitis. To put it simply, these infants have more complicated symptoms that include vomiting blood and aspiration of food contents into the lungs. They could be at risk of failure to thrive.

A little more science: digestion, reflux and treatment

When we eat, food passes down the gullet (oesophagus) into the stomach. Cells in the lining of the stomach make acid and other chemicals which help to digest food. Stomach cells also produce mucus which protects them from damage from the acid. The cells lining the oesophagus are different and have little protection from acid.

There is a circular band of muscle (a sphincter) at the junction between the oesophagus and stomach. This relaxes to allow food down, but then normally tightens up and stops food and acid leaking up (refluxing) into the oesophagus. In effect, this sphincter muscle acts like a valve.

Advice for parents of children with acid reflux is initially to nurse or feed babies in an upright position. It would also be advisable to try and keep your hands away from their tummies while winding them, so as not to put too much pressure on their little bellies.

If this is not helping much, many people use a thickener in their feeds (for example Gaviscon, which is available from pharmacies), but again I recommend that you seek advice from your GP, public health nurse or pharmacist about what is best for your baby.

The next phase of treatment involves referral to a paediatrician for assessment. Depending on the severity of the reflux disease, your child may require medication for partial or full acid suppression. These medications can reduce – either fully or partially – the levels of acid being produced by the stomach. They may be required for several months. However, they are not recommended for long-term use. The stomach needs acid for various reasons, and it is not a good thing to suppress its production for too long. Regular consultations and follow-up appointments with your paediatrician are advised for a considered, gradual reduction in the dosage of these suppressants.

Occasionally, as you will see in the case study 'John's story', babies with reflux symptoms may require an endoscopy (camera study) directly into the gullet and stomach to see what is going on inside.

Symptoms of paediatric GERD

- Pain, irritability, constant or sudden crying which doesn't subside or can even get worse as the day goes on.

- Frequent spitting-up or vomiting.

- Vomiting or spitting-up more than one hour after eating.

- Projectile vomiting – the type where even the walls and floors aren't safe!

- Refusing feeds or accepting only a few ounces even though showing signs of being hungry.

- Poor sleep habits; inconsistent and frequent waking.

- A 'wet' sound when the baby burps.

- Baby halitosis! Stinky (acidic) breath.

What follows is a case study about a child with reflux. The reason I have included this here is that I consider reflux to be a medical condition that needs to be fixed before there is any intervention with sleep problems. While you are waiting for the reflux condition to settle down – or indeed you suspect that your child suffers from reflux and you want to try and get some relief – perhaps this story will help.

Case study: sleepless nights (and days) with a baby suffering from reflux

John's story

Louise's first child had suffered from GERD or acid reflux and was diagnosed at four months old. She presented with a range of symptoms, such as fussing with her bottles, projectile vomiting that was clearly causing her pain, an acidic smell on her breath, and the obvious issues with sleeping. She would only sleep upright and would scream the house down from around 5 p.m., which was when the acid build-up from the day would become too much for her. She was prescribed a medication named Losec MUPS and was a different baby afterwards. The family never looked back.

So, when John was born and started to show early symptoms of reflux, Louise was well-equipped to deal with it. Or so she thought.

John was diagnosed at four weeks old: his reflux was silent, but he was experiencing 'wet burps', which were clearly hurting him as he grimaced in pain. His parents were all too familiar with the acidic smell from his breath. He also cried a lot and pulled his legs up to his chest as though he had bad trapped wind. He was a 'fussy baby', and they had difficulty feeding him and maintaining his weight.

For John's parents, the most difficult part – along with juggling life with a toddler and a newborn – was that he wouldn't (or couldn't) sleep. He would be awake for most of the day and it was hard to get him settled at night, although while they were waiting for a diagnosis Louise tried all of the sleep tips for a baby with reflux (listed below), which she feels definitely helped. (I can't stress enough how important it is to use these tips if you suspect reflux. Follow them, regardless of whether you have had a diagnosis or not. Your instincts will tell you if there is something going on with your little one.)

Once diagnosed, John was prescribed Losec, and his feed was changed to an anti-lactose feed called Nutramigen, as lactose intolerance can be linked to reflux. Delighted, Louise thought that this would be the silver bullet it had been with her daughter. But unfortunately this was not the case.

John's treatment helped temporarily, but he started to deteriorate again. At three months old he stopped taking his bottles altogether. He would only have to see the bottle coming and he would howl the house down. Louise bought every different bottle on the market, and tried feeding in a light room, a dark room, with the TV on, with it off, with music on and with music off. The only way she could get any milk into him was when he was asleep – a permanent dream feed scenario (see 'The dream feed', p. 64)! This worked for a couple of weeks, but then he began to refuse it, even in his sleep.

The only thing he would take was water. John's parents ended up in Accident and Emergency at the hospital with him and were referred for tests. Poor baby John had an abdominal scan, and a 'barium swallow' procedure was performed to show what exactly was going on in his digestive system when he fed. Unfortunately, the results weren't good. He had a very severe case of GERD and oesophagitis, which meant that the acid had burnt his oesophagus, which is why he refused to eat. He was prescribed a different regime of medication and, once again, his feed was changed to a weighted feed called Enfamil A.R. Finally, after two weeks, John started to feed again.

During this time Louise and I had been in contact, and we were able to sort out a feeding and sleeping pattern for daytime that suited the family. Despite Louise's requests for sleep coaching, we decided to wait until we were sure John's reflux was under control before we started on that.

John was almost ten months old when we finally decided the time was right. Overall, they haven't looked back and have had only a few nights when John has been unsettled. But his sleep disturbance was mainly due to teething at that stage and they all got back on track in no time!

Tips to help with reflux

- Elevate the head end of the cot. You can do this by either buying a wedge that sits under the mattress or blocks that go under the legs of the cot.

- Use a 'sleep positioner'. The less babies with reflux move in their sleep, the better. The more they move, the more the contents of their stomach move, which is what you want to avoid. A sleep positioner is like a small, thin foam mattress, which has two adjustable and removable bumpers on the side. It is more often used to help prevent babies from rolling onto their tummies, but can also help with babies with reflux, as their arms can rest at the top of the bumper, encouraging a straight-back position.

- Swaddle your baby (as mentioned earlier).

- Consider side-sleeping. I know I am slightly contradicting myself here; safe sleep guidelines recommend putting babies flat on their backs to sleep. A baby with reflux will experience pain in this position. I imagine for them it is like having heartburn; lying on your back can only exacerbate it and is very uncomfortable. (I'm not saying that reflux and heartburn are the same, but that is how I would imagine this type of pain.) Many babies will be more comfortable sleeping on their sides. Yes, babies are at lowest risk of SIDS sleeping on their backs. They are at most risk while sleeping on their tummies. Sleeping on their sides is the middle ground. But there is not enough statistical evidence to state that side-sleeping poses a greater risk. To reduce the risk of them rolling onto their tummies, use a sleep positioner (as mentioned above), which restricts their movement while still allowing them to be more comfortable.

- Try to find an 'anti-colic' bottle. The less trapped wind your baby has, the better. Most brands have a specific anti-colic range. Louise used MAM bottles for feeding John and loved them, having gone through pretty much every type on the shelves.

- Make sure you sit your baby upright after each feed, in particular the last feed before going to bed, for as long as thirty-five to forty minutes if possible. Baby doesn't necessarily have to be awake, just upright.

- If you have things to do (and who doesn't, right?), use a baby sling or a baby carrier after you have fed your baby to keep the little one upright. John would frequently sleep in this during the day. *Avoid* using a bouncy chair – this aggravates the issue, as your baby is more likely to throw up. Invest in a chair in which your baby can sit more upright.

- Increase the frequency of feeds and give less milk. Babies are more likely to throw up if they are too full. So give less food in smaller quantities, more often.

It is so important that you try not to get overstressed at this time in your baby's life, no matter what issues you are encountering. Be good to yourself.

Tiny babies, more than anything, need love. They need cuddles and feeding, and then more love. Your newborn has come from your womb, which is the safest place in the world, and the first instinctual needs are for security and survival. Enjoy your tiny baby. They don't stay that way for long.

2

FOUR TO SIX MONTHS

You did then what you knew how to do, and when you knew better you did better.

Maya Angelou

Over the first few months you will see that life with your new baby changes almost daily as the little one grows and develops. By four months of age your baby will be smiling at you and will become more expressive and vocal. He or she will react to your face and voice and start to have those delicious little conversations of 'nonsense' with you.

Physically, your infant will be much stronger and, by now, will be beginning to master head control. At this time babies will start to hold their heads up when engaged in tummy time. Some babies can even roll from their fronts to their backs at this point. Generally, babies at this stage will not roll from their backs to their fronts, so there is usually no fear of them doing this during the night or during naps – yet!

Many babies start to sleep for longer periods at night, even up to six hours at a time, which is great news for parents – but again, don't stress if your baby doesn't do this. This simply might not be your baby's 'normal' just yet.

Feeds: what is 'normal' at this stage?

At around four to six months old, your little one will probably still be feeding at three- to four-hour intervals (including night feeds). But by this age your baby will have managed to adjust to an understanding of day and night, and will spend the majority of the hours between 7 p.m. and 7 a.m. in the 'land of nod'. However, bear in mind that when managing a transition to a new developmental stage your little one may need extra milk, so don't withhold this, even if you have had an apparent routine in place up to now.

Bottle feeding: four to six months

Between four and six months you will surely see a pattern developing. Baby will start to take feeds at regular four-hour intervals, give or take half an hour either side. Up to six months of age you will see your little one's intake increase to approximately 6 fluid ounces (180 millilitres) per feed.

The dream feed

A dream feed should happen about three to four hours after baby goes down for the night. It is a simple feed, whereby you lift the little one and offer a breast or bottle feed. The beauty of this is that, if you want to, you can go to bed early, and then – at around 10.30 or 11 p.m. – dad, on his way to bed, could offer this feed from a bottle. In this way mum can sleep uninterrupted for up to seven hours, without having to feed during the night.

Put simply, this 'dream feed' entails picking the baby up while he or she is still asleep, offering a feed, and then placing the baby back in the cot with as little disruption as possible. More often than not, babies don't really need to be winded after this feed, as they are quite relaxed and barely aware of it even happening. For children aged around six or seven months and older, I would suggest not even changing their nappy at this time, as this can rouse them – and you definitely don't want that happening!

Some babies can be extremely sleepy when you lift them for this 'dream feed', and parents often worry that they are not managing to get them to drink enough. It can be difficult to encourage them to drink, or indeed latch on if you are breastfeeding, and they can be equally as determined not to drink from a bottle.

Tips for rousing, without wakening, your baby

- Stimulate the inside of the baby's cheek with the teat of the bottle to encourage your baby to start sucking. Touch baby's lips with your nipple if you are breastfeeding.

- Take a piece of cold wet cotton wool and wipe it along baby's jaw line.

- Gently reposition your baby in your arms to slightly rouse the little one without waking baby fully – just enough to notice the first signs of sucking or drinking.

- Rub baby gently on the cheek or chest.

Some typical feeding schedules and a simple routine

When things are going well, there is no need to change anything, but sometimes, maybe due to a regression or growth spurt, your baby's feeding habits will change. He or she may start to take more food, or start to feed less. I am going to suggest some typical feeding 'schedules' and also propose a simple routine that I like to use for babies from four to six months old, before the introduction of solid food.

With breastfed babies it can be more difficult to find a 'typical' pattern, and it is more likely that 'anything goes'! I believe you will find a rhythm, in tune with your baby, over time.

Sample routine for a four-month-old

You might at this stage consider putting a little 'shape' on your baby's day. Remember, the amount of food and feeding times are flexible. If your baby is hungry, you *must* feed him or her. In my opinion, withholding food is not an option; you *have* to be flexible. Don't wait until the scheduled time if you think your baby is hungry – just feed the little one. In terms of naps, at this stage your baby should start to be able to stay awake for up to two hours or so before getting restless again and needing a sleep.

7.00/7.30 a.m.	Wake and feed/bottle
8.30 a.m.	Sleep (one hour or so)
10.00–10.45 a.m.	Play
11.00 a.m.	Feed/bottle
12.00 noon	Sleep two hours + (this is the most important sleep of the day and should be in the cot – try not to have it here, there and everywhere!)
3.00 p.m.	Feed/bottle
4.00/4.15 p.m.	Sleep (wake by 5.00/5.15 p.m.)
5.30 p.m.	Short feed if breastfeeding
6.00 p.m.	Start winding down for sleeping (bath, massage, cuddles)

7.00/8.00 p.m.   Feed/bottle and bed*

10.45/11.00 p.m.   Feed/bottle (dream feed)

Many four-month-old babies will not yet be ready to have their bed-time at 7 p.m. For a few more weeks, at around 7 p.m. they may drift in and out of a light sleep, and perhaps won't settle for the night until around 9 p.m. This is perfectly okay and normal. So, don't be concerned if they are not having an official bedtime at 7 p.m. just yet.

You will see from the schedule that unless you are feeding on demand, your little one might start to stretch up to three-and-a-half to four hours between feeds.

And yet, just when you think you have things under control, some babies might start to experience a few setbacks with their sleep. You might have had a sleeping angel, but all of a sudden things change and your baby starts waking more frequently. Or you may have a little one who was never a great sleeper, but who seems to get even worse. Wouldn't it be great if there was a reason for this? And some helpful advice? Well, luckily, there is!

Sleep regression at four months

During your child's first few years it is normal for him or her to go through periods when it feels like things are starting to go backwards, or even just not really progressing, in sleep terms. You may look for reasons as to why things have changed at around this four-month mark and ask:

- Is my baby hungry?
- Have we not established good habits?
- Should we sleep train?

The answer to the first two questions is, quite possibly, 'Yes'. There's a good chance that you have been doing perfectly fine in terms of positive habit-building, but your little one is changing and growing fast. Babies will usually have easily doubled their birth weight by now, and will be growing further by the day. All of these changes, along with other new developmental stages in their lives, are bound to impact on their sleep pattern.

The answer to the third question is still 'No'. Babies are simply too young to start a training regime at this time, but it may be a good time to start having a little more structure in their day, as I discussed earlier in the chapter.

Now, back to the idea of sleep regression.

By now, your little one will probably be sleeping up to sixteen hours in a twenty-four-hour period – usually eleven to twelve hours per night and a number of naps during the day. Three to four naps would be normal.

At around four months of age there is a lot of growing and learning going on, and often, when there are big developmental changes, sleep can be disrupted. As babies learn new skills like rolling, sitting, crawling, standing and walking, it is as though they practise them over and over in their heads even in their sleep until they have accomplished them. Once they have mastered them, sleep returns to normal – until the next milestone approaches. Then, unfortunately, it can start all over again! This is why you hear of the nine-month and twelve-month regressions, during which sleep can again be affected negatively as babies start to crawl or, indeed, walk. These growth spurts will happen sporadically during the first few years, but this one – at four months – seems to be the most obvious and the one commented on most by parents. (By the way, it doesn't happen at exactly four months to the day. It can occur anywhere from three to five months.)

Recognising the signs

A few signs may alert you to this regression in your baby:

- Babies may be a bit 'off' and not as happy in their environment as before. Some would call it 'increased fussiness', but I think 'off' describes it well!

- They may be more likely to rouse frequently at night. For example, there may be hourly waking after midnight where before they were managing a long stretch and were able to sleep until 4 a.m.

- Their naps can become a little fractious. Often, too, they won't take them all, even though they may have done so quite happily for a few weeks before. They may go from sleeping for long stretches during the day to being 'cat-nappers', only catching half an hour here and there. I will talk about naps separately, at the close of chapter three, as they can be the bane of many parents' lives!

- They may change their feeding habits. Some babies will start to feed badly during the day and drink all night. You end up in a catch-22 situation: they aren't hungry enough to bother with feeds in the daytime as they have been having their fill overnight.

Responding to the signs

I suggest that you muddle your way through these phases with a lot of patience and deep breaths. Recognise that it is probably just a regression, and that it will pass, like most other phases. But there are ways to help make it easier for both of you:

- Accept it for what it is – a disruption and not a disaster.

- It may sound hard to believe, but this too will pass.

- If you have to, go back to rocking or comforting, which you may have done when your baby was very tiny. It will not be the end of the world and will not last forever. Remember, these babies will need comfort from you more than anything.

- Provide plenty of extra cuddles and calmness. Offer emotional security, as these regressions can often coincide with periods of anxiety for little ones. Separation anxiety often rears its head at this stage too.

- Give your little one extra opportunities to practise the new skill. If your baby is learning to roll, offer lots of tummy time. Get down on the floor with baby and give encouragement.

- In short, go with the flow as best you can. Keep a diary if you need to, and try at least to keep the bedtime consistent at around 7.00 or 7.30 p.m. This will ensure there is something familiar for your baby at the end of a potentially tough day – by that I mean tough for everyone!

Weaning breast to bottle

There will come a time when, for whatever reason, you will want to stop breastfeeding your baby. Some mothers continue for many months, even years, while others simply 'know' at what point they would like to wean their baby from the breast. Of course, you do not need to stop breastfeeding just because you have introduced solid food to your baby's diet, and it is worth remembering that your little one will need either breast or formula milk until at least the age of twelve months.

However, you may need to return to work, or have other practical, emotional or physical needs that require you to wean your baby off the breast. So here I'm going to give some handy hints to help you make this process as painless as possible. I have tried and tested these with parents. However, I am not a breastfeeding expert, so I would recommend that if you are struggling with the idea of stopping and would like professional advice, then talk to your public health nurse and see what advice is offered. There are lots of fabulous breastfeeding support groups in Ireland, too, both in your local area and also online.

Timing is important

It is important to find an appropriate time to start weaning. It is not a great idea to start weaning when, for example, there is an upset to your baby's routine – such as teething problems, a holiday, guests staying, or even a house move! Life-changing events and special circumstances can be quite disruptive for a little person and will only make your weaning job harder. At times like these it is best to maintain the status quo. (This applies to making other changes too, for example getting rid of a soother when your child starts playschool. It is probably not the right time for him or her when so much change is going on.)

Take one step at a time

Unless you have been instructed by your medical practitioner to stop breastfeeding quickly (perhaps due to illness or before being admitted to hospital), the weaning experience should feel like a process rather than an all or nothing, 'do or die' event. Your baby will be able to cope with this change if you approach it while remaining tuned in to his or her needs.

Cut down on the breastfeeds gradually. For example, at the beginning, pick one feed to omit. It is probably best not to drop the first one in the morning or the last one at night, as they can have a particular emotional significance for everyone. Do without this one 'dropped feed' for a good few days, preferably a week, before proceeding to drop another one.

Express

Express milk if you can, in order to minimise your own physical discomfort at this time. You can freeze it, of course, and in this way your baby can have your milk in a bottle – maybe from dad – and this 'bridge' towards the creation of some distance between you and your baby can be further supported in a healthy way.

However, do not express more than you need to while still being able to feel comfortable physically, as your breasts will keep producing the same amount of milk. Be careful if you are deciding to night wean and feel that expressing might be a way of approaching this. You may confuse your body, as it will continue to produce milk because it thinks you still need it. You should try to express a little though, as otherwise you could become engorged and run the risk of developing mastitis. A wise breastfeeding mum once told me that drinking sage tea can help to minimise your supply and lessen the risks of overproduction of milk when you are trying to cut back on feeds.

In short, the longer the time you have available to you to stop, the easier it will be on your body, both physically and, indeed, hormonally.

Ask for help

You will need the support of your partner at this time. If your partner has already been giving your baby bottle feeds (perhaps of expressed milk, or of formula), then the chances are that weaning will go more easily and become less of an ordeal for everyone involved, especially baby. By doing so, your partner will already have helped to communicate to your baby that it is not only you who is able to provide feeds.

To stop giving a bedtime feed from the breast, it can be helpful to ask your partner or a relative to take over the management of bedtimes for a while, so as to introduce a 'new' bedtime routine.

Offer substitutes

If your baby is under twelve months old, don't forget that he or she will need either breast or formula milk to satisfy nutritional needs, so do try to encourage your baby to take a bottle/cup of formula or expressed milk. Many babies refuse to drink out of the bottle; actually, that can be viewed positively, as it is then one less thing for your baby to become dependent on!

Some parents find it's best to just go straight to a sippy cup. Chances are the baby has been drinking water from one up to this point anyway. Again, I repeat, don't force the bottle on your baby. This doesn't have to be the only alternative to breastfeeds.

The art of distraction

Fully weaning from the breast is not necessary if you simply want to night wean. But, if you are looking to make permanent changes and finish breastfeeding altogether, then the art of distraction might help. You will already be a dab hand at distraction techniques, and this will be a really good test of your abilities! Go out, start walking, visit the park, or take up swimming. In short, do whatever it takes to pass the time! Less time to think about breastfeeding can only be a good thing when you are weaning your baby from the breast.

Sitting down together and 'doing nothing much' only gives your baby an opportunity to think about, and look for, a nuzzle and a feed.

That's not to say, 'Stop the cuddles!' though – they just might have to be limited for a while and well compensated for at other times. Time for cuddles will always need to be built into your day with your baby.

Your baby needs all the love in the world at this time. This is a big change for your little tot, and you will want to minimise any feelings of insecurity or vulnerability at this time.

If you are finding this process of weaning your baby from the breast difficult, do not hesitate to seek support and guidance.

Tips for weaning

- Babies become self-aware and quite discerning as to what they do and do not like from as early as two months old, although this is more likely to become obvious at around four months.

- Don't wait till your child is hungry before trying something new like offering a bottle instead of a breast. Your child will handle new experiences when in good form, content and well rested.

- Offer the bottle during a 'dream feed'.

- Offer the bottle with the baby on your knee, rather than lying down across you, and begin to feed with the baby facing outwards.

- Let your little one play with an empty bottle in order to get used to the feel, look and smell of it.

- Perhaps have the milk in the bottle slightly warmed.

- Your child's mouth is wide open when he or she is feeding from the breast, so try to fill the mouth with the teat as much as you can. The 'tommee tippee closer to nature' bottles have a great-shaped teat, and many people find transitioning to this shape can be quite successful.

Moving your baby into his or her own room

The best time to start the move out of your room and into the baby's own room is when the baby is younger, rather than older. As I stated earlier, most of the official guidelines recommend that you and your baby sleep in the same room until the little one is six months old. Many will have made the move before this for various reasons, but most people wait until the six-month mark. There are some babies who are simply 'noisy sleepers' and are 'evicted' quite early on. (I don't believe that parents who decide to make the move early are doing anything wrong. They are usually just being quite practical and simply want everyone to have as good a night's sleep as possible!)

The longer you leave it, though, the harder it is going to be to remove your baby from his or her recognised place of sleep. Also, as your baby gets older and more aware of their surroundings, chances are you are waking them as often as they wake you. You may grumble or groan in your sleep just as the baby switches from one cycle to another, and, hey presto, baby is awake! The little one thinks you're up and it's party time! Noooooo!

Having said this, *you* have to be ready too. It is your choice. Don't feel bullied or pressurised into moving your baby unless you are ready.

As an 'in between' or transitional step, and depending on the size of your bedroom, you can start to move the cot away from its close position at the side of your bed. You can edge the cot gradually further away from you and head it towards the door! If your baby is going to be sharing your room for a while, however, due to space restrictions at home, then a good place for the cot is at the foot of the bed. You are far enough away for your infant not to be able to see you directly and yet near enough should you need to tend to your little one during the night.

The important thing, though, is to make sure that the place where your baby is going to sleep at night, alone, is comfortable, safe and familiar. If you haven't already done so, you could try to put your baby in the cot in the new bedroom for the daytime snoozes, so that baby learns to feel secure in this new sleeping environment.

Eventually, you will manage to move your baby fully into his or her own room. Spending a lot of time in the baby's bedroom with the baby, especially during wind-down time or the last bedtime bottle/feed time, can also help the little one to feel comfortable and relaxed.

Some parents might choose to wait in the room with their baby until he or she falls asleep, while others may prefer to leave the room. Sometimes it is argued that staying with babies as they fall asleep is making a rod for your own back. The logic behind this is that if your baby needs you around in order to fall asleep, then they will expect you to be there when rousing, even briefly, later on. And if the baby wakes up during the night, it might be difficult for the little one to fall asleep without his or her 'association', which is *you*!

In the end, however, it is up to you to find out what works best for you and your child, particularly as you go through a period of change.

Twins and multiples

It's all well and good to talk about sleep when there is only one baby, but it would be a bit remiss of me not to mention sleep issues for twins and multiples too. Although the situation can sometimes become so complex that it could be said that they deserve a book of their own!

Although twins are often described as 'double the trouble', this is not always the case; many parents of twins and multiples make their way through the sleep minefield with few or no issues. But often the simple fact that there's more than one baby looking for you and needing you strikes fear into everyone! The best advice I can give you is to accept help when it is offered. Often, after the birth of a single baby, when dads go back to work, mums are conscious of dads needing enough sleep at night, so they take over the majority of the responsibility overnight. With twins and multiples that luxury is essentially gone. It's a matter of having all hands on deck!

Remember, twins and multiples might have come into the world together, but they are individuals. Therefore their developmental stages may not always occur at the same time. It is important to bear this in mind, because it can often be hard to plan routines in advance as the babies may each have different needs at different times. They may have arrived a little early and, therefore, you have to take this into account when it comes to milestones.

Many identical twins will have pretty much the same sleep patterns. It is more likely for non-identical twins to display greater differences in the manner in which they sleep. Their little, developing personalities will be a key factor in deciding on how you manage their sleep too. However, it is a good idea to try to get them into a similar feeding and sleeping pattern as soon as you can. Whether you are breastfeeding or bottle feeding, it might not be feasible to try to feed them at exactly the same time, but within half an hour of each other is advisable. If one twin wakes in the night for a feed when they are still newborns, it is advisable to feed the other immediately afterwards. This will also help you to avoid forgetting which of your babies you have already fed – feeding during the night can cause things to become a bit of a blur!

Naps and night-time with twins

The same 'rules' apply when encouraging good sleep habits and sleep routines for all babies, regardless of whether there is one child or more than one. Your daytime will be busier, but structure can be really beneficial, as you will be less likely to end up confused. Without it, you may end up asking yourself, 'Who did I feed?' or 'Who hasn't slept well?'

Trying to achieve and maintain the same naptime for both babies will also enable you to get some well-deserved 'time off' for yourself – if there ever really is such a thing!

In the early days the babies will probably fall asleep straight after a feed, but once they start to be a little more wakeful after feeding, put them into their cots for their naps whilst they are still a little awake – drowsy, but awake. This is exactly as recommended for all babies at the various ages and stages of development.

Overnight

You may find that you are lucky enough to have two good sleepers! But if you don't, you will need to decide which baby to tend to first.

More often than not one baby will look for more from you than the other. You may have one noisy baby and one baby who is generally a little calmer. My advice, if they both wake during the night and don't need feeding, is to tend to the calmer baby first. Make sure the first twin has settled before attending to your little noise-maker.

Separation anxiety and sleep regressions

It should be noted that separation anxiety can happen at any stage in your child's first few years. Some babies or toddlers barely blink when their parents or carers leave them. It is not that they are more secure little people than others; it's just that they are independent little souls and know that they are safe wherever they are and whoever they are with! So don't beat yourself up if your little one shows signs of being slightly anxious when you leave them. It's not necessarily you – it could be them!

Separation anxiety is a pretty dramatic, but often normal, part of growing up. Sometimes it can seem to appear out of nowhere, and your usually easy-going small person will suddenly develop fears over your departure.

Children may have been looked after by someone specific, or may even have been attending crèche for some time, before separation anxiety starts. Sometimes they may even start to develop attachments to one parent rather than the other. Dealing with it and *not* ignoring it is the best thing we can do for them.

Helping with separation anxiety

Pre-empt the early stages of separation anxiety by having regular carers in your baby's life. This might mean grandparents, aunties, uncles, babysitters or friends. Don't have too many long goodbyes – your baby will sense your unease and will react accordingly. Fake it if you have to! The initial tears will soon dry (for both of you!) and, while it can be unnerving for parents, it will pass, so try not to take it too personally.

Normally separation anxiety will happen just as you start the transition to something new – perhaps as you think about going back to work. You will be checking out your childcare options or gradually settling your little one into crèche and you may start to notice a 'clingyness' creeping in. As if this is not tough enough to contend with, this anxiety can also affect baby's sleep habits. They may become poor nappers, or begin to resist the actual naps themselves. It's not irrational – they may feel that they are being abandoned each time they are put down for a nap, and who can blame them? Provide comfort and reassurance. Stay with your baby if needs be while they fall asleep. If it helps the baby feel secure during this period of change, just be there.

I will mention toddlers' separation anxiety issues later on in the book when we deal with that age group.

Time goes by so quickly in the first few months of parenthood.

It may feel like no sooner than you have just begun to get to know your bundle, along comes a new phase in their little lives. Over the next few months, you will see them take huge leaps – both physically and developmentally – and they become almost grown-up with the introduction of solid food. It's time to travel a new road with your baby – a time where you will possibly see the most change taking place.

3

SIX TO TWELVE MONTHS

A goal without a plan is just a wish.

Antoine de Saint-Exupéry

By six months, your baby's gross motor skills will have really developed. Some babies of this age may be able to sit up on their own, or even crawl. Their hand–eye coordination will have improved and they will be able to distinguish between familiar and strange faces. If you have managed to follow the routine from the last chapter you should find that your day is starting to take on a recognisable pattern, with eating and sleeping times fairly consistent.

In this chapter I will describe some routines for a baby from six to twelve months old, and also look at realistic expectations around baby sleep at this stage. With many mums finishing up maternity leave after six months, lack of sleep can become an even more pressing issue than before. It's not too late to start putting a plan in place.

The importance of sleep and a daily routine

The word 'routine' is often bandied about by many parenting experts. It can strike fear into the hearts of parents, who will say, 'I don't have a routine', or 'How do I start a routine?', or 'How do I get a routine that works for the rest of the family?'

But routines don't have to be regimental and boring. They don't have to limit your freedom. You will have time to do all the things you formerly did and still want to do. Sometimes parents get so bogged down in the details of a routine that they can end up limiting themselves with too much structure and not having enough fun. I want parents to have a good life too! A routine should be easily manageable, and really all that is needed is a schedule with fairly structured and regular feeding and sleeping times. I often say to parents, 'If you get five days out of seven on the right track, then you are doing great.' Make allowances and have some days off. That way you will still manage to achieve your goals without feeling too restricted.

Putting more structure into the daytime hours of your baby's life can have a very positive knock-on effect at night. You may be quite surprised at the close relationship between these two elements of a twenty-four-hour day. More structure and more consistency in establishing helpful routines will give parents and babies boundaries to work within. These boundaries will provide limits for little ones and their parents, and will help to create posi-tive associations with naptime and bedtime. Increased feelings of security and comfort will go hand in hand with boundaries.

Now, let's get back to that dreaded word 'routine'!

The routines that worked well for me over the years when I ran my child-minding service have been tried and tested to good effect. All the babies that I cared for were able to slip nicely into the same routines I outlined for their parents even before they joined me in The Nursery. By being always mindful that parents need to 'have a life of their own', I truly recognise a place for flexibility. Parents will always be able to catch up with a little adjustment of lengths and timings of sleep, should things go a little bit askew during the day.

Sample routine for a six- to eight-month-old (including three solid meals per day)

7.00/7.30 a.m.	Wake and milk feed
8.00/8.30 a.m.	Breakfast (3*)
9.00 a.m.	Sleep (forty minutes maximum and wake by 10 a.m.)
11.00 a.m.	Milk feed
11.45 a.m.	Dinner/lunch (the main meal of the day) (1*)
12.00 noon/12.15 p.m.	Sleep in cot – up to two hours
2.30/3.00 p.m.	Milk feed
4.00/4.30 p.m.	Sleep (wake by 5.00/5.15 p.m.)
5.30 p.m.	Tea (lighter meal than lunchtime) (2*)
6.00 p.m.	Start winding down (bath, massage, cuddles)
7.00/7.15 p.m.	Milk feed – 7 fluid ounces (210 millilitres) – and bedtime
10.45 p.m.	Dream feed – 7 fluid ounces (210 millilitres)

1, 2 and 3 indicate steps for starting solids. Start by offering a spoon-feed at the 'dinner' time first, that is 11.45 a.m., then after a week or so introduce a second spoon-feed at teatime. After a further week to ten days, start to offer a third spoon-feed at breakfast time.

At this stage your baby should start to sleep in lengthier, more solid blocks at night. Some babies can settle themselves between sleep phases and this will give you up to eleven hours of unbroken sleep. But the normal run of events would see little ones rouse briefly during the night. You may need to go in to them for a quick resettle or to offer a soother, but hopefully nothing more. In order to reassure yourself that your little one is not waking out of hunger, I recommend that you offer a dream feed before you go to bed yourself.

Continue with this dream feed until your baby is around seven months old or at least well established on solids.

Note: The times in this sample routine do not have to be exact, but are based on a 7 a.m. to 7 p.m. schedule for most babies. I am a little flexible with the times for sleeping and feeding, and would recommend that you follow these simple structures while remaining flexible. Managing everything roughly within an hour of the set times will be fine. I would recommend that you wake your little one before 10 a.m. to make sure that he or she goes down for the 'big sleep' at around midday. Also, in the evening I wouldn't encourage your baby to sleep much past 5 p.m. so that you can have a good two to two-and-a-half hours of awake time before bed, somewhere between 7 and 7.30 p.m.

Before we look at further schedules for slightly older babies, I'll cover some important points about feeding and sleeping at this stage.

Feeding (solid foods)

Dinner is the main meal of the day for these babies, so it should include plenty of vegetables and protein. Try to get good amounts of green vegetables into their diet at this stage, as their natural store of iron starts to diminish and will need to be replenished.

I suggest that babies have their main meal at lunchtime, rather than later on. When babies, and even older children, have had a good breakfast and a good lunch they will have the necessary 'fuel' to feel well and feel full all day, which helps to avoid the tendency to snack unhealthily throughout the day. It also means that they will not go down to sleep for the night on a tummy full of dinner along with the last bottle or breastfeed.

So for tea I normally recommend a lighter meal, for example fruit and yoghurt. I say this because although you want them to have eaten enough, you don't really want them falling asleep on too full a tummy. (I know myself, if I have had a heavy meal in the evenings I find it hard to settle as continuing digestion runs counter to my body relaxing.) Giving your baby the greater amount of food earlier in the day will help to rule out digestion problems and mild discomfort, and the possibility of trapped wind from a heavy belly at bedtime.

The routine or schedule for babies at this stage of development can look a little bit 'busy', and although it may seem as though you will have no time for anything else, in practice it is pretty easy to get into the swing of things once you start putting it in place. I know many mums will still be on maternity leave at this point and might want to have a few breaks, lunch dates and so on; as a result, it's not the end of the world if your little one sleeps in the buggy or pram at lunchtime on the odd occasion! (Just maybe not every day.)

Milk feeds

Breastfeeding

You can see from the routine I gave above that I suggest five milk feeds a day, including a dream feed, for babies at six to seven months old. Many breastfed babies will naturally drop some of the daytime feeds and will not be looking for feeds as regularly as they may have done previously. It is hard to say exactly, but I would estimate that a breastfed baby who is well established on solids would be having three to four feeds by day, and two or more overnight.

For many Irish mums, this age range may coincide with going back to work; you may be deciding to reduce daytime feeds for this reason. Generally, if you wish to continue feeding while you return to work, it doesn't mean that your supply will dry up. For as long as you are feeding (even small amounts), you will still be able to produce milk. If you are finding that your supply is diminishing, one idea might be to try to express a little at some point during the day in order to encourage your supply to continue.

As I mentioned above, for most breastfed babies I would still expect at least two to three feeds during the night (between bedtime and morning – 7 p.m. and 7 a.m.).

Bottle-feeding

Once your baby has started solids (at six months) I would expect a maximum of five bottles of 6–7 fluid ounces (180–210 millilitres) in a twenty-four-hour period (including the dream feed). From around nine months old, your baby will, I hope, be well established on solid foods and perhaps be having a few finger-food snacks during the day. I usually recommend at this age that they are having three bottles of 7 fluid ounces (210 millilitres) during the day and, ideally, no feeds after bedtime.

As I have mentioned before, there may be times when more feeds will become necessary, in particular during this first year. Such times could be when little ones are going through a growth spurt, or indeed if they are teething. Believe me, these phases will pass and normal service will resume before long.

I suggest that from around seven months old, and when your baby is well established on solids, you stop actually adding up in your head the amount of milk your baby drinks. Let baby take what he or she needs or wants, within reason, and leave it at that. Offer drinks of water too, to prevent any possibility of dehydration. You can get really caught up in counting ounces and it can nearly drive you mad! Even if you are establishing a routine for your baby, you still have to be flexible. We all have hungry days and not-so-hungry days. Babies are no different. There's a lot of change going on and, as I have pointed out, you will need to monitor these changes as they occur and be prepared to adjust to meet the needs as they present themselves. Feeding amounts are unique to each child, whether breastfeeding or bottle feeding. Once your child is thriving and gaining weight, all will be well. It's a question of trying to remain attentive, sensible and flexible! As babies start to eat solids, and as long as they are drinking plenty of water, we can begin to rule out hunger at night as a cause of waking.

It is important also to note that feeding and sleeping are two separate activities, and, where possible, are best kept that way. Children very quickly make associations between the two. For example, if children fall asleep while drinking a bottle or while feeding at the breast, they can become confused, as it's the last thing they remember when they wake and when it's not there in the middle of the night they may have difficulty getting back to sleep without it. This also applies to naptimes during the day. Try to avoid feeding to sleep (whether with breast or bottle) once your child leaves that newborn stage, so as to avoid any potential poor sleep aids.

Dropping the dream feed

Once your baby is eating well and is fully established on three meals a day, you can try dropping the dream feed (see p. 64). There are two ways of doing so:

1. Simply decide one night not to give it and hope for the best. You may be pleasantly surprised!

2. Gradually reduce the amount of formula you give your baby at this feed, over the course of a week. So if you started by giving your little one 7 fluid ounces (210 millilitres), on the first night reduce to 5 fluid ounces (150 millilitres); on the second and third nights reduce to 4 fluid ounces (120 millilitres); and further reduce on the fourth and fifth nights to 2–3 fluid ounces (60–90 millilitres) and then nothing.

Sleeping

Sleep aids and sleep associations

We have now established that the first step towards encouraging better sleep is to introduce a daytime routine to give structure to your baby's day and ensure your little one is getting sufficient naps at the right times during the day, as well as creating a separation between times for sleeping and times for feeding. The next step you can take is to consider the difference between sleep aids and sleep associations.

Quite often, just knowing the difference between sleep aids and sleep associations will set you on a path of encouraging good sleep habits with your baby.

Sleep aids

The term 'sleep aid' describes all of those objects or props you use to get your baby to go to sleep. In general they are physical or tangible things. These can be products like musical mobiles, lights on the ceiling, and special teddies with vibrations or white noise.

The term also includes the physical things a child might need to fall asleep, including being rocked or walked around, having a bottle/breastfeed before nodding off, enjoying motion in the car or buggy, or, in some cases, pulling at mum's hair to fall asleep! This latter ploy may be soothing for baby, but pretty painful for mum!

Sleep associations

Sleep associations are those things that help your baby to think, 'Oh! I am expected to go to sleep now!' They are usually subtle, and can be as simple as the last words you say to them, for example 'Goodnight sweetheart, I love you', or the 'special kisses' and other night-time rituals for your baby or toddler.

Young babies and children of all ages learn by repetition, so consistency at bedtime will be the key ingredient in your recipe for forming good patterns of sleep behaviour. Adults, children and babies will wake at intervals, every night. This is completely normal. The aim of the 'good sleep habits game' is to teach your baby or older child to settle back to sleep while needing very little or no assistance from you!

I prefer to rely more on sleep associations than sleep aids to encourage good sleep habits, particularly once your baby hits the six-month mark and you may be considering a little sleep training. Allowing your wakeful and restless baby to be in control of sleep habits is really no use to anyone. Your baby won't have the required hours of sleep per night – eleven to twelve hours – for healthy development. Just as importantly, you won't get enough sleep to rest and recharge your batteries, and this can have negative consequences for your wellbeing and relationships within your family.

Tips for encouraging good sleep habits

- Always try to get babies down into the cot while they are still awake. Try to make sure that your baby wakes up if the little one has fallen asleep during the last feed, be it breast or bottle, before placing the baby in the cot. Even if your baby is not fully awake, simply watch that the baby's eyes flicker so you know the little one is not fully asleep. Use the time spent winding down at the end of a feed to rouse them a little. The reason for doing this is so that babies are awake enough to know where they are going. This prevents them feeling confused later when they wake up, and as far as they will then be aware, they fell asleep in your arms and have woken up somewhere else. When this happens it can be unsettling, and even disturbing, for your baby. Your baby will wonder, 'How did that happen?' I believe that might be potentially a scary feeling, so the idea here is to avoid it happening in the first place.

- Ensure that babies have good feeds at the end of the day. By this I mean that your child will have a full bedtime feed (as well as a dream feed until he or she is well established on solid foods). For older babies and toddlers, their tea and bedtime bottle should be enough, but it's not unusual, and can be helpful, for parents to offer older babies a little snack before bed.

- Do not worry if your baby grizzles (which I'll discuss in the next section) when initially being put down into the cot. The little one may simply be creating his or her own version of 'white noise' and be trying to block out other sounds around, which may be comforting before getting into the sleep zone.

- Use a soother at the beginning stages of sleep. Do not continually put it back in your baby's mouth because you think he or she might wake up! Only use it as it is intended – as a soother. A soother should be used to calm babies and help their breathing pattern slow down to a restful and steady rhythm. Although a soother is a sleep aid, it is also a very reliable tool as a sleep association. It is one of the only things I know that acts as both a sleep aid and a sleep association tool. Where possible, in between feeding and sleeping, do not give your baby a soother (although I do understand that there are times when this policy can cause a battle – or when you just need five minutes' peace! – see chapter 4 for more on soothers and sleep coaching).

- Maximise the difference between day and night by using lights and curtains to your advantage. Invest in blackout blinds or use black plastic refuse sacks to darken your baby's room. Darkness stimulates the production of melatonin, the natural hormone linked to sleep. Although your newborn may previously have slept anywhere, bright or dark, your six-month-old will have more awareness of what there is to miss out on and may find it harder to nod off during daylight hours. Therefore it is a good idea to provide a darkened room for your baby, at naptimes as well as during the night.

- Help your baby to develop his or her own internal body clock. Our body clocks are based on a need, or 'drive', for sleep, which ebbs and flows over a twenty-four-hour period. This ebbing and flowing is called the circadian rhythm (internal body-clock), and this regulates timings between periods of sleep. A six-month-old baby will normally have an urge to sleep roughly every two-and-a-half hours after rising in the morning. For example, I expect a six-month-old to get up at 7 a.m., nap at 9.15/9.30, nap again at 12.00/12.30, and probably once more at 4 p.m. Then bedtime will be at approximately 7 p.m. You can encourage the development of a pattern like this by setting the scene at naptimes by darkening the room and giving your baby an opportunity to sleep. Interestingly, an average adult will have a strong urge to sleep between 2 p.m. and 4 p.m. each day. Our European neighbours manage this well through their enjoyment of an afternoon siesta!

- The bedroom should be exactly what it says on the tin – a bedroom. It should be a peaceful place and should be maintained as a bedroom, not a playroom; when possible there shouldn't be too many toys or clutter to stimulate the little one at sleeptime. This will allow your baby to learn to go to sleep alone, naturally. Babies are not born with a need for 'stuff'. It is not conducive to the development of good sleep habits. It is often parents who create this 'need' by providing too many play materials for their children and, worse still, offering them at the wrong times, for example DVDs in the middle of the night if your toddler won't sleep! My father used to tell us that our bedrooms were a reflection of our states of mind (regularly messy)! Think calm and peaceful, rather than busy and sleep-free.

- Check the temperature of the bedroom. I recommend keeping your baby's room cooler rather than warmer, as it is often easier to keep babies warm than to cool them down.

- Once bottle-fed babies are weaned onto solid foods, at approximately six months, they should be able to manage to get through the night without feeds. They may initially have one dream feed at around 10/11 p.m., but this can be excluded once they are well established on solids. Breastfed babies are more likely to have two or more feeds overnight (actual feeds, and not just for comfort). You will see that I have said 'get through the night' not 'sleep through the night', as it is important that you remember there is a difference between the two!

Grizzling

Grizzling is the sound that your baby makes shortly before falling asleep. In tiny infants I describe it as 'mooching noises' – a little murmuring sound as they get into their sleep zone. As children get older they may still be grizzling, but it can sound as though they are crying a little, so be careful not to interrupt this grizzle. Leave them to it.

I liken grizzling to that moment when you yourself are about to fall asleep. You are fumbling around in your bed, maybe finding your 'cold spot' or comfortable position just before you nod off. Your partner might notice this mooching and decide that as you are still awake, it is a good time to ask you something. As you know, this can be really annoying! So apply this logic to disturbing your baby just as the little tot is about to nod off because you think he or she is still awake – grizzling! If you constantly go in to settle your baby because in your mind the little one is not settling, and baby is simply grizzling, you will in fact be disturbing them. *Listen* carefully to your child.

More sample routines you can follow as the months pass

As your baby gets older and more active you will need to tweak the routine a little. If you have followed my six-month routine up until now, you should find this transition quite seamless. Here is my suggestion for your eight- to ten-month-old.

Sample routine for an eight- to ten-month-old

7.00/7.30 a.m.	Wake and milk feed – 7 fluid ounces (210 millilitres)
8.30 a.m.	Breakfast
(Maybe a short nap between 9.15 and 9.45 a.m.)	
10.30 a.m.	Snack and water
12.00 noon	Dinner/lunch
12.30 p.m.	Sleep in cot (up to two hours – no longer)
3.00 p.m.	Milk feed – 7 fluid ounces (210 millilitres)
4.00 p.m.	Snack and water
(Maybe a short nap between 4.15 and 4.45 p.m.)	
5.30 p.m.	Tea (lighter meal than lunchtime)

6.00 p.m.	Start winding down (bath, massage, cuddles)
7.30 p.m.	Milk feed and bedtime

You will see now that the morning and evening nap can occur in a more haphazard pattern. I recommend that you try to stick with the morning and lunchtime nap at this stage, and if baby does not sleep later in the afternoon, then it is not such a loss. In the absence of the afternoon nap your baby may be more tired than usual at bedtime, so it may be advisable to bring bedtime back by half an hour or even an hour earlier than usual, to avoid the dreaded overtiredness. I mention later in the book about how being overtired can be counterproductive.

If your baby is breastfed, from around ten to twelve months your little one should be able to manage a twelve-hour period at night with only one to two feeds, although many mums may have decided, for whatever reason, to night-wean by this stage. As long as your baby is thriving and gaining weight, and obviously not waking just for feeds, then this is fine too.

At this stage changes to the routine are subtle and we should bear in mind that each child is different. You may find that some little ones will start to cut back on naps and also on milk feeds, but by twelve months their day should be looking something like this:

Sample routine for a baby of twelve months and older

7.00/7.30 a.m.	Wake and milk feed
8.30/9.00 a.m.	Breakfast
(Tiny fifteen-minute nap if really exhausted!)	

10.30/11.00 a.m.	Snack and water
11.30/11.45 a.m.	Dinner/lunch
12.30 p.m.	Sleep in cot (up to two hours)
2.30/3.00 p.m.	Milk feed*
4.00 p.m.	Snack
5.30 p.m.	Tea (lighter meal than lunchtime)
6.00 p.m.	Start winding down (bath, massage, cuddles)
7.30 p.m.	Milk feed followed by bedtime

Sometime around twelve to fifteen months, many bottle-feeding parents will decide to knock this feed on the head. Once they have done this, they might stop the morning and evening bottle feeds and offer cups of milk instead, but I would suggest that by eighteen months, your child should definitely not be having an afternoon bottle. It is quite a personal choice and, in my opinion, there is no real problem with babies having bottles as they become toddlers, apart from potential dental issues as time goes on.

You will see from this schedule that I don't expect little ones to nap in the morning at this stage. This can be a little tricky to manage initially, as your baby gets used to being awake for longer periods of time. However, if the little one really needs it, allow and encourage your baby to have a little cat-nap, for around ten to twenty minutes (but no longer), at around 9.30/9.45 a.m. You will still want them to go down for their main nap around midday. You can gently rouse them and use 'snack time' to distract them on awakening. Once your baby begins to show little interest in this nap, or it becomes difficult to get them to nap mid-morning, then you should consider dropping it completely.

If, after twelve to fifteen months, your little one is eating well and still waking for a breastfeed, I would be starting to assume that this feed was more of a habit than for the specific reason of hunger. At the same time, I do think that if your well-fed baby, who is more than eighteen months old, is still waking for feeds during the night, the little one might not just be unusually hungry. Instead, your baby may be experiencing a slight sleep problem or, at least, using you as a 'crutch' to fall asleep again! If this doesn't bother you, by the way, there's no real reason to change anything, is there? Comfort needs (and comfort feeds) are important too, and some mothers find that they can accommodate them even in the middle of the night.

The routine given above will remain the same until children start to grow out of having a need for a midday nap altogether. And you will see that, by around two-and-a-half years old, they will no longer need it. Should your little one start to fight bedtime, it is time to drop the nap during the day. This can apply to toddlers as young as eighteen months old, and if this happens with your child, ensure a slightly earlier bedtime to counteract the absence of a nap during the day. You can either go 'cold turkey' on the mid-day nap by just deciding to drop it one day, or you can gradually reduce the time spent napping over a period of one to two weeks. For the record, I prefer the second option.

Back to sleep, briefly: a word on napping

Naptimes are wonderful – for babies and parents – when children sleep for as long as they are 'supposed' to. It is all well and good for me to tell you that your child should nap for a block of two hours during the day. You could get stuff done and know that your little one is getting enough sleep!

But what if they don't nap well? What if your little one seems to be a cat-napper, catching half an hour here, there and everywhere during the day? Throughout the day, as children slip from an active sleep cycle into a deeper sleep cycle, some can have a little difficulty settling between the two stages. So they wake fully and are picked up. They get used to this and so never really learn the art of resettling themselves during the day. Hence they become cat-nappers.

One way of managing this is to really try to follow and maintain a routine (like the one I have laid out above), and to wake your little one from the morning nap to encourage sleeping a little longer at lunchtime.

There are lots of babies who seem to nap quite well and even for a long period in the morning time. This might suit many people if they are picking up an older child from school at midday, but a problem can arise where they sleep too early in the day. They may not be tired enough for a nap in the afternoon and then they can be overtired at bedtime. This can lead to frequent waking before midnight, as they can't seem to be able to get into a deep sleep. They can be 'jumpy' and active in the early part of the night and generally might not settle well. If you see this happening with your baby, then I would discourage a lengthy morning nap.

Another good idea is to try to rouse children a few minutes before they normally wake. So, if your baby sleeps for exactly thirty minutes every time, without fail, you could gently rouse the little one after twenty-five minutes, and place him or her back down in the cot again. It is known as the 'Wake to Sleep' technique.

My advice for dealing with a cat-napper is not to stress too much about it. If you are trying to encourage your baby to take a longer nap (for example the midday nap), I recommend that you attempt to resettle baby for at least fifteen to twenty minutes. If, at that point, the little one is showing signs of falling asleep, then continue to ride it out. If not, then forget about it and get on with your day. Your baby will probably have a 'catch-up' nap later on.

Don't worry, though. For some babies, it is simply their 'normal', but it is definitely possible to turn your cat-napper into a long-napper over time.

And, if you are considering some sleep coaching with your little ones, be aware that settling for naps may not come together for you quite as quickly. Naptime settling can take a little time to fall into place, but bear with it.

4

SLEEP COACHING:
IS IT FOR YOU?

It is such a mysterious place, the land of tears.

Antoine de Saint-Exupéry

If your baby is over six months old, well established on solids and still waking several times a night, you may feel it's time to take action. I have heard many new parents say, 'Oh, I just get used to surviving on a few hours' sleep at a time.' This may be acceptable for adults in the short term, but babies shouldn't be allowed continually to have less sleep than they need.

You are in a position to teach your baby to sleep better and longer, through encouragement and gentle guidance. Babies will learn that rather than being abandoned to fend for themselves, they are being steered towards a new behaviour. It can be the difference between enjoying good quality sleep and just sleeping from exhaustion. I must repeat, though, that sleep training is *not* for everyone, and the decision to engage with it is very personal for every set of parents.

If you decide to use specific techniques to help your child to go to sleep and sleep soundly afterwards, it is important that once you have started, you see it through. Otherwise your baby will get mixed messages and your goals will not be achieved. Not only will it be confusing for your baby, but it will give your little one an opportunity to test boundaries in an unhelpful way. The nature of this approach relies on firm, decisive strategies, but you should still be sensitive to your baby's needs. I am not for a moment suggesting that you leave your baby to cry for extended periods of time. You must still meet their emotional needs for comfort and reassurance. A little flexibility, therefore, will be needed.

Sleep is a natural process, which is why, once the basics are learnt, you will have given your baby the help he or she needs to develop his or her own capacity for self-soothing, and the gift of sleep itself!

The phrases 'self-soothing' or 'self-settling' in the context of little ones' sleep mean a baby's ability to fall asleep without much assistance from a parent/carer or the likes of bottles/feeds. (Soothers themselves are indeed considered aids in terms of sleep, but I generally don't count them as a sleep crutch. They also mean that babies can resettle themselves to sleep without assistance when they wake between sleep cycles at night.) If you are finding that your baby is struggling to get off to sleep, then it simply means that your little one has yet to master this skill and we can help the child learn to soothe themselves, with a little time and patience.

A baby's inability to self-soothe can be one of the reasons why they may experience ongoing sleep problems.

The causes of sleep issues

There are always underlying reasons that explain your child's sleep pattern. Your child may or may not ever have been a great sleeper, but the good news is that there are solutions to most sleep problems that may arise! As I have mentioned, often the primary cause of sleep problems is babies' inability to self-soothe – to put themselves back to sleep when they experience the normal brief awakenings during the night. This usually occurs because they have become over-reliant on a sleep aid (the physical presence of someone, bottles, breastfeeds, rocking, etc.) and need it to get back to sleep.

Here are ten of the most frequently occurring issues that may negatively impact on the development of healthy sleep patterns. Bear in mind, though, that they do not always create problems; if, for example, your baby is falling asleep on a bottle and still sleeps until morning without problems, then leave things as they are!

1.   Your child needs to be rocked or sung to sleep.

2.   Your child has become over-reliant on a soother.

3.   Your child has developed the habit of falling asleep on a bottle at naptime and at bedtime, or your breastfed baby has developed the habit of falling asleep at feed time.

4.   You have an older child and for fear of waking him or her, you react too quickly when your baby wakens.

5.   Your baby is still in your room after six months.

6.   Your little one is not getting enough sleep during the day. Strange as it may seem, overtiredness is often a real problem.

7.   You do not have a fairly well-established sleep routine during the day.

8.   You try anything and everything to get your little one to sleep, but give nothing a decent chance to work. We all learn by repetition, but babies learn nothing from a mix of events during the night.

9.   Your child is hungry. Remember, we are talking about babies older than six months when we are considering sleep training, and at that stage they should be taking solid food as well as milk feeds.

10. Your child simply doesn't know what is expected of him or her at bedtime.

Rituals and other random oddities

Before we delve into some of the sleep-coaching challenges I have encountered in my practice, it might be a good idea to lead in gently and lighten things up with a giggle. A sense of humour can play an important role in any baby-management strategy. It will prevent tension from building up and the situation becoming out of control!

To that end, here are some of the more unusual situations I have come across during my time as a sleep coach. Some of these puzzled me, some made me laugh and some I found, quite simply, odd. I even thought that some couldn't possibly be true!

Most people enjoy indulging in their own personal little rituals before getting into bed and falling asleep. These can be conducive to creating a good atmosphere and a good attitude for sleep. Others can be more counterproductive.

My own personal preference is listening to the radio. I listen to anything from current affairs to sport commentaries – just anything, really. Sometimes I wonder if any of the information is absorbed, because I suspect it's more about the sound of a human voice than the content of a programme. If I took in even a fraction of the information I listen to each night I'd probably, by now, be the wisest person on this planet. But, seemingly, it is the sound of the human voice that leads me towards nodding off – and not the content at all! But I am an adult and I am able to fall asleep without it. I just prefer it (and I don't need it turned back on when I wake up during the night!). I do not recommend any music/ sounds for little ones during a sleep-coaching process.

Hair pulling

Holly, 10 months old, loved pulling her mum's long hair before she fell asleep. If she had to, she would have a go at her father's hair – but it was much shorter and therefore less satisfying to pull on, so more often than not her mum needed to be close by at bedtime.

Unfortunately, Holly's mum's hair began falling out, so an alternative calming practice was called for. We came up with an experiment, where her mum agreed to wear a really tight, latex swimming cap at bedtime for a few nights, so that the option of pulling hair was removed. After just a few nights of this wonderful fashion statement being brought into the mix, Holly no longer sought to be settled in this way. She started to settle, and resettle by herself during the night, without the need to pull on her mother's hair.

Hand holding

Luke liked to hold a parent's hand before nodding off. This habit is more common than you might think. Some babies, and even some older children, like to hold onto mum or dad's hand before falling asleep. This in itself is not such a big deal as long as it doesn't take hours at bedtime, but sometimes little ones need to rehold a parent's hand when they wake during the night.

Along the same experimental lines as in Holly's case, we introduced a scratchy, woolly glove; Luke soon learned to stop looking for a hand to hold, and the physical contact, in order to fall asleep.

Ear rubbing

Later on you will read a case study where I discuss the trials and tribulations of a four-year-old boy, Marcus, who had never spent a night in his own bed. Yes, you read correctly: never!

This little boy was not only unsure about where he should sleep, but his 'go-to comforter' was either of his parents' earlobes! He would reach up and rub them as a baby, and he held on to this as a comforter, even as he got older. I don't think he actually cared who the ears belonged to – any babysitter's ears would also do!

This was only a part of the problem with Marcus' bedtime, and you will see how we managed to solve his bigger issues later on (see Case Study: 'The big boy bed hopper', p. 188).

Motion

In another case study, you'll meet a little toddler, Sophie. She could fall asleep only while being pushed around in her buggy. She loved being wheeled around the hall at night before going to sleep. This would not have been too difficult for her parents if she had then proceeded to sleep until morning, but she woke frequently during the night. Her parents would have to go back downstairs, put her into the buggy and do a few more laps!

Sophie didn't expect this to happen in her crèche (and happily slept in her crèche cot). We therefore knew she was capable of settling herself. Her parents really did not know how to change this ritual. But soon enough, by changing the situation at bedtime, the ritual was forgotten (see Case Study: 'The wheeling wonder', p. 109).

Massage

Something my own niece, Ava, used to love was having someone rub their fingers up her back as she relaxed. She called it 'rubby on my back'. It wasn't necessarily a sleep association for her, but to this day (she's now six years old), if we are sitting down to watch a movie, she will often just look up and say, 'Rubby?'

This same niece, as a tiny newborn, used to love to settle into sleep in my arms, with her head dangling below the rest of her body. Not upside down or anything, just slightly angled towards the floor. She's perfectly normal now – and doesn't sleep like a bat!

Being the mini-boss of the house

During my time as a childminder, I discovered that one of the little boys I looked after, aged ten months, used to 'demand' that his parents take turns to lie on a mattress on the floor of his bedroom, all night! I only discovered this one day when his dad arrived at The Nursery almost doubled over in pain, having spent the previous night sleeping on the floor with his arm dangling into the cot at an awkward angle. The little guy was perfectly happy to nod off on his own in the cot during his time with me at The Nursery!

It was a bit of an eye-opener not only for his parents, but also for me. He was one of the children who inspired me to investigate the sleep world of a baby. It's funny, though: when I mentioned to his mum that I would like to share his story in this book, she laughed and said, 'Gosh, I barely remember that at all!' I realised again that it is amazing how we quickly forget issues when they resolve – particularly when they were once crippling!

Evicted parents

I have encountered many children, in the course of my work, who need their parents to lie with them at bedtime. Some babies, and older children, need their parents not only to 'come lie with me', but also to stay all night.

Many parents stop sharing a bed for this reason. One parent is either evicted to the spare room or ends up in the baby's room, while 'junior' occupies the parental bed for the night. These little ones, in turn, end up languishing in the master bedroom with one or other parent. I recall visiting a house where 'Dad's Room' was beautifully decorated with 'princess bed linen' and 'princess wall-paper' – happily the lads at his work didn't see it!

But this problem is not limited to children in their parents' bed. There are parents who nightly hurl themselves over the bars of their baby's cot, as baby refuses to sleep alone. In these cases, it happens because parents are insistent that they will not bring the baby into their bed so as not to create bad habits. But surely this is worse! It's a matter of 'out of the frying pan and into the fire'. This solution is not wise, safe or comfortable!

Case study: the wheeling wonder

Sophie was around ten months old when her parents got in touch with me. They were exhausted, as their little girl expected to be pushed around in her buggy for at least half an hour before bed. As if this wasn't enough of a pain, she also wouldn't go back to sleep when she later woke without being whipped downstairs and back to the buggy for round two. And rounds three, four and five (and so on)! Did I mention that her mum was also five months pregnant at the time and was beyond exhausted, and also dreading the thought of this continuing with a newborn on her hip?

We met one evening when Sophie had gone to bed. Then, right on cue, she woke and I was able to see exactly what stages mum and dad had to go through to get Sophie to go back down again.

Sophie attended crèche on a full-time basis, so she was in a pretty good daytime routine. Occasionally she fell asleep in the buggy on the way home, but it was only for around ten minutes. That was not a big deal as far as I was concerned. Sophie also napped well in crèche, without the buggy, which was frustrating for her mum and dad. Still, we know that children often 'play' one parent off against the other, so the same can apply with crèche versus home!

The main problem was the buggy and Sophie's reliance on it to fall asleep at bedtime and throughout the night. It was purely an association with her house, and she expected her parents to go through these motions each night. It had been so long since her mum or dad had tried to settle her in the cot that they were pretty anxious about starting the process. With a little guidance and reassurance, they decided to try it.

Sophie woke one further time before I left. I did not suggest that they start that evening with the technique I had shown them, as they hadn't run through it at bedtime and I felt that would have been a little unfair on Sophie.

Night one went relatively well (although maybe Sophie's mum and dad wouldn't agree!). It took Sophie an hour-and-a-half to settle. She was awake again at 3 a.m. Her dad went in, and it took almost as long for her to settle. At this time, Sophie's mum was wondering if perhaps Sophie's teeth were bothering her. It is not unusual for parents to look for other reasons as to why their child is not settling, but I feel it is important that once you start some training, you try not to stop (unless the child is feverish/sick/quite obviously in pain).

Night two was better. Sophie still woke later on, but she settled back to sleep much more easily.

Sophie woke only once on night three and managed to settle back to sleep with very little assistance from mum or dad.

Night four was tough all over again. This is a perfect example of the 'kick-back night' (see chapter five, p. 148). It was tough, but they made it through.

Within ten days, Sophie was doing brilliantly. Her pregnant mum was getting rest and the house became a happy zone once again. The buggy was brought out only when they went for a walk!

More sleep facts

Here are a few things to bear in mind when you embark on a new bedtime/naptime format, some of which I have touched on already when talking about helping with pre-sleep routines:

- Nobody sleeps through the night. We all – babies, children and adults alike – wake during the night, but we are usually able to go back to sleep without much bother. Perhaps just a flip of the pillow will do and we are asleep again. So it is not this fictitious holy grail of sleeping through the night that we should be aiming for. Realistically, nobody sleeps for twelve hours straight through, without waking at some point or another. A really solid block of sleep would actually be around five hours! Most children, and many babies, actually have this, but what is at issue is their inability to go back to sleep without parental support when they wake between sleep cycles. This is what we want to work on and, ultimately, help them to achieve. We can confuse babies and small children when we are helping them to resettle – this is especially so when we combine too many strategies, including picking them up, rocking them, shushing, giving a soother, giving a bottle, etc., but rarely doing the same thing twice. The aim of the game is to deliver one consistent message: it's time to sleep!

- The ideal bedtime from five or six months of age onwards (some babies will manage this at four months) is between 7 p.m. and 7.30 p.m.

- Bottle-fed babies on three good solid meals a day should not require any further bottles during the night. They may want them for comfort, but not because they are hungry. By allowing your bottle-fed baby to drink bottles late at night, or throughout the night, you may end up establishing habits that are difficult to sustain. Find an alternative way of settling baby, even if the little one initially becomes cranky and a bit cross. Once you are delivering the same message, your baby will soon get used to the fact that there is no bottle forthcoming and, more often than not, they will forget about it within a couple of nights.

- The last thing your child does before going to sleep is often the first thing they remember when waking. Should your child fall asleep in your arms or with a feed or bottle at bedtime, the little one may want the same 'treatment' every time he or she wakes at night. It's not the child's fault, just a habit children become used to. But, as the saying goes, 'If it ain't broke, don't fix it.' Many of the issues associated with settling children, such as rocking or staying with their children, are not problematic for a lot of parents; it is often a question of how helpful versus how disruptive parents find any given settling method.

- Siblings can share rooms very successfully. This might surprise you, but quite often they are very happy having each other around at bedtime. They will see it simply as quite normal and even quite nice!

Is sleep coaching for you and your family?

Sleep coaching – or sleep training as it is also known – will not be right for everyone, and it doesn't always guarantee a sleeping baby after a number of nights. But it will usually have a significant impact on your child's sleep habits and it can be of huge benefit to a family struggling to cope with sleep deprivation. It will offer your baby some new understanding and a change of expectations around bedtime behaviours.

Settling babies and encouraging them to nod off by themselves can become a real sticking point. As I outlined earlier in this book, with sleep coaching you can explore your understanding of sleep aids like music, feeding, rocking and the like, and see if perhaps the things you are doing to encourage sleep are in fact the cause of the sleep disturbances.

Quite often, even a slight adjustment to your daytime routine, and a few changes at night, will have a positive impact on the challenges that may have thwarted bedtime/overnight sleep up to now. I recently met a mum who mentioned that her six-month-old was sleeping very badly during the night, but would sleep for hours on end during the day. It seemed, in fact, that he was oversleeping and had his day and night mixed up a little. Although his mum was more usually a *laissez-faire* person and had no real structure in the day, she agreed to try to implement a daytime routine. In twenty-four hours her little guy had gone from fifteen wake-ups per night, to just waking once for a little reassurance and falling straight back to sleep. I asked her how she felt about the changes and hoped they weren't too restrictive. She remarked that now she could predict what might happen next and was able to make plans to meet people based around her little one's new sleep schedule. Before this, she simply didn't know what might happen, or when!

Commitment to the principles of sleep coaching is important. Some mums and dads do themselves no favours by rushing headlong into sleep coaching without considering the need for commitment or indeed, fully understanding the techniques. You will set up serious barriers to achieving improved sleeptime goals if you do not consider the commitment and hard work necessary for change. It is the parents themselves who do the work of implementing change. Having a sleep coach come into your home to assess your situation, to explore the factors specific to your baby's sleeptime and to support you in following through with change is, for most parents, of untold value. Parents I have worked with will testify to this – I have included some testimonials at the end of this book (see appendix two). They are always so kind and grateful, and yet I have to remind them that it wasn't me who made the changes. They did. They should be proud of their work and their successes. They were not mine! (But of course, I am always very happy to hear of successful outcomes.)

Sleep training doesn't always mean night upon night of tears and drama. The methods I use involve parents fully. The focus is on guiding babies towards different behaviour at sleeptime and teaching them new skills to help them to settle before sleeping all by themselves.

Sleep training is not for everyone and you should not feel pressured into doing anything that doesn't feel right for your family. Many families are happy simply getting on with minor sleep struggles. Quite often, however, a time comes when what might have been working for a while simply stops being effective.

Things to watch out for before considering coaching

If you are thinking of doing some training with your baby, and they have reached six months of age, there are a few things I would suggest you keep a close eye on, as making changes to these issues might solve your sleep problems without the need to employ a sleep coach.

Overtiredness

Many babies can tend to wake quite soon after going to bed. This can often be the result of the baby being overtired at bedtime. Have a look at your baby's daytime routine. Quite often, putting a little bit of a structure on the day can have a very positive knock-on effect at night. Ensuring that baby is getting adequate sleep during the daytime hours, along with sufficient stimulation, fresh air and enough food (a mix of solids and fluids) will all be pointers for you when it comes to working out why your little one's sleep may be disturbed at night.

Overstimulation

Maybe you are doing too much to get your child to sleep in the first place, and therefore either confusing or overstimulating the little one. Examples might be rocking baby, pushing baby in a buggy or indeed letting him or her fall asleep on the bottle. If babies are not aware of where they are when they first go to sleep, it can be very confusing for them when they rouse after that first sleep cycle.

Room sharing

If, at this age, your little one is still sharing a room with you, chances are you are disturbing baby just as much as baby disturbs you. Now is the time to make the move.

Still no improvement?

If all else has failed, it might be time to try coaching. I have put together a brief checklist to help you decide if it's for you.

Checklist to decide if the time is right for sleep coaching

If you can answer yes to most of these, then the time is right:

- Is your baby fighting daytime naps?

- Is your baby fighting bedtime?

- Does your little one wake on numerous occasions during the night, and not just for a soother?

- Does your baby stay awake during the night for long periods (more than thirty minutes at a time)?

- Is your little one reliant on bottles or feeds during the night to nod off?

- If breastfeeding your baby, are you ready to night wean?

- Do you feel that you have tried everything and nothing is working?

- Are you exhausted?

- Is your relationship with your partner beginning to suffer?

- Are you tired of hearing about everyone else's child who sleeps amazingly well?

- Do you feel that your world is consumed by 'all things sleep'?

- Are you prepared for a little crying while you make a change?

- Are you staying put for a time? No holidays coming up? No period of change?

- Do you feel you can commit to a process for a few weeks?

Timing and other considerations

Quite often, timing is important – both for your baby and for you. I'll discuss this consideration here, and also cover a few other key ones.

The six-month mark and solid-food meals

Your baby must be at least six months old and well established on solid food for sleep coaching to be optimally helpful. That way we can start to rule hunger in or out as a cause for waking. At the six-month stage, three solid-food meals per day, along with approximately 28 fluid ounces (800 millilitres) of breast or formula milk, will ensure that your baby will not be hungry during the night.

The health of your baby

Your baby must be healthy – and not badly teething. When your baby feels well, adapting to change is easier. I'm not saying that a healthy baby will accept change without a fuss, but I certainly wouldn't put babies under any further stress when they feel unwell. It's common sense, really.

Obviously, if your baby has an infection, a cough or a cold, the little one's waking may not simply be because of poor sleep habits. Babies will need some comforting at night if they waken feeling unwell. Wait till they are better 'in themselves'. Use your instincts if this is the case before thinking about making changes to sleep routines. You know your own child better than anyone. When your baby recovers and feels healthy again, try to achieve one or two good daytime sleep experiences. Then you can consider starting your training by exploring your baby's sleep issues and introducing helpful changes to their sleep routines.

Teething is a personal issue, really. Some babies seem to teethe with some difficulty, others less so. You will very quickly learn a lot about your baby's teething process when you observe your child's reaction to the advent of each new tooth. If your baby struggles, then hold off on training until you find some respite in the teething process. Talk to your GP or public health nurse if you have concerns about other possible underlying medical causes for your baby's sleep disturbance. You may even want to consult a paediatrician to check your baby's health.

Your own health
Parents should be feeling well too. If you are completely exhausted or not feeling 100-per-cent well you will find it harder to commit to a new process. See if you can have your baby minded for a night or more before you begin training, so that you are firing on all cylinders when you start.

If that is not possible, consider beginning some training over a weekend or at a time when you will both be at home for a few days – thus using 'parent tag team time' to catch up on lost sleep during the day. If one of you has to get up early every day it can give you a reason to give in, and you will end up feeling disappointed after making an initial commitment.

Agreement between partners
Equally as important as your health is that both you and your partner really have to be on the same page. Both of you must want to do sleep training. If babies sense tension or unease between partners, they will be pretty quick to pick up on it. Don't worry about having to leave your baby to cry. There may be some tears, but the tech-

niques I use do not let baby cry without you being physically present to comfort the little one. Get together and talk about what you want from this and communicate about giving support to each other. Sleep training will not work if you don't work together, as you need to provide your baby with a joint, clear and consistent approach.

Emotional support

Having someone to support you emotionally is a key positive influence. If you are parenting alone, it might be a good idea to ask a good friend or family member to stay with you for a couple of nights so you will have the emotional support you will undoubtedly need. Trying to sleep train your baby without emotional support is more difficult, but not at all impossible.

I recommend that partners put increased focus on being good to each other, and ask for the same in return, as they begin sleep coaching with their baby. If you are finding it tough and need your other half to take over, just ask. In other words, before beginning agree to ask for and accept help offered by your partner to ensure the best results. Knowing you have someone who has your back will keep your spirits up. In the same way, don't be a martyr! Use your back-up person, who will want to help.

Night weaning if breastfeeding

If you are breastfeeding your baby and feel that the little one is using the breast only to fall back to sleep rather than for a feed, you may want to consider night weaning in order to start to put some sleep coaching in place. Your baby may not be hungry as such, but is used to having feeds in order to resettle. But as breastfeeding forms part of a very special relationship for many mums and babies, these wakenings might not be a problem for you, especially if they are relatively short feeds and your baby falls asleep again quite easily and quickly. A good night's sleep and breastfeeding are not always mutually exclusive.

In terms of sleep coaching, by still offering feeds sometimes and then using a resettling technique at other times, you could make things too confusing for your baby. Therefore, I am hesitant to recommend sleep coaching for a baby who is exclusively breast-fed, unless you are ready to night wean. Once we can start to rule out hunger as a source of waking during the night, many mothers will be happier to night wean. If you are not ready to night wean, then sleep coaching is probably not the best option for you for now. Perhaps, if you are not already doing so, you could try offering a dream feed at about 10.30 p.m.

The window of time you will need

Give it time. The night training itself will take approximately four to seven nights, but give yourself a window of at least two to three weeks for the new structure to settle more fully into your baby's life. For example, don't do any training before a holiday or before the arrival of a new baby, as these will be disruptive to the process.

In short, if you have any upcoming 'life events', plan around them accordingly. 'Lie low' if you can during any training.

Crying

Although my techniques do not include 'controlled crying', I do expect that there will be some crying, but it will be more as a result of frustration, as your little one won't be getting the expected 'normal' reaction from you (I will talk further about crying in the

'Your questions answered' section which follows). This crying will not damage your baby, because you will be there with baby as the adjustment happens. Neither will it last forever.

I prefer that parents feel that they are central to this comforting process, rather than leaving it to babies to work it out for themselves. This 'crying stage' of the process is usually very short-lived.

What other people might think

Don't start worrying about what other people might think of you doing this. Remember, each to their own! People who are up at night with their little ones, but are happy to be so, won't understand why you would want to make changes. Sleep coaching is a very personal choice. Don't worry about your neighbours hearing some crying. As I mentioned already, the crying will be short-lived, and we have all put up with party nights next door!

If there is a genuine concern, talk to them. Let them know that there may be a little disruption for a few nights. You have enough going on; it isn't necessary to be worrying that the neighbours might think you are neglecting your baby, so try to put this issue to bed (excuse the pun!).

Seeing changes

If you decide to use the help of a professional sleep coach or are intending to use the guidelines in this book, keep a notebook handy, or use the sleep diaries section at the back of this book, to record what goes on during the night, and keep your partner updated with this process. It is often encouraging to look back and see changes as they happen. Trust me, if you follow these guidelines, positive change will occur before long.

Making allowances for developmental reasons

Acknowledge that your baby's sleep disruption may simply be a response to a developmental transition, for example learning to crawl or to walk. Make allowances for this, but from my experience long-term sleep problems are more often *not* caused by these issues. They may have started because of a developmental change, but – more often than not – they quickly become habitual. Sleep problems are probably not 'just a phase', as phases pass, but sleep issues are those that last longer than a few weeks. If you regularly find yourself in this position, it could be time to do something about it.

Your questions answered

Will there be any crying?

The short answer is yes. There will inevitably be some crying with any kind of sleep training, but you will see that, when using my proposed technique, mum or dad will always be present in the room with their child if the little one is upset. Crying is almost always involved, but it is generally no more than a protest against the new regime. Babies and older children develop expectations around sleep and will react to changes. For example, if you have been rocking baby to sleep for some time, the little one will have begun to expect that this will continue to happen. Once you decide to stop rocking your baby, he or she will, as you would expect, react.

Crying is a form of expression and a form of communication and should not be ignored. Your baby's tears can tell you that something is amiss – for example, crying can tell you baby is hungry or has a pain.

Crying can also take the form of a response. Your baby will let you know that he or she recognises change. Initially, baby may not enjoy changes to routines that are, for now, comfortable – but these routines may not be in your child's long-term interests, nor in yours. Perhaps the reason you are reading this book is because your baby's sleep routines are disruptive and uncomfortable for you.

Change is inevitable. Such is life. And how we react to it is just human nature – humans cling to what they know. Show me a person who loves change! You may be starting new schedules and techniques at naptime and bedtime, and I suspect that most children will object to these changes. I want to remind you that sleep training is not all about 'crying it out'. In my opinion that method implies a battle of wills and can set up other difficulties. For me, sleep training involves sensitivity to your baby's personality and needs, coupled with consistent, and often somewhat strategic management techniques.

Yes, there will some crying, but it will bear the hallmarks of understanding and resolution rather than those of a battleground. Sleep coaching will accommodate age- and stage-appropriate sleep schedules. And you will be following a tried and trusted child-centred path, with your baby's interests always at the heart of things.

How long will it take?

How long is a piece of string? It is difficult to predict exactly how long the process will take, because there are so many dependent variables. If sleep training fails, the main reason is inconsistency, which results in your baby receiving mixed messages. I usually suggest to parents that sleep coaching will take four to seven nights, but I ask them to allow a window of two to three weeks before everything can be expected to settle down.

What about 'attachment parenting', and babies who are allowed to sleep in bed with their parents?

Shortly I will be taking a quick look at 'attachment parenting', part of which encourages bed-sharing. Unfortunately, sleep training really does not work quite so effectively when a child sleeps in your bed and you are happy that this particular arrangement continues. How could it work? Babies will have a tough job learning to settle themselves if a parent is lying there beside them, as this interferes with teaching the baby to learn the important skills associated with self-soothing.

My job as a sleep consultant is to quickly and effectively help baby and the whole family sleep well, with as little disruption as possible. The methods I recommend to my clients would not work quite so well with 'attachment parenting' families.

Having said that, if you are a co-sleeping family by choice, and everyone in the family is well rested, sleeping safely and happy with the sleeping arrangement, there is obviously no need to change your sleep situation. Strict attachment-parent families will believe that the child will move out when THEY are good and ready, so they rarely have an issue with having them in their beds. Parents practising attachment parenting will rarely use a sleep coach or go down any sleep training route anyway. Once again: 'If it ain't broke, don't fix it!' Oh, and if it is broken, it *can* be fixed!

Attachment parenting

Attachment parenting, as described by Dr William Sears and Martha Sears in *The Baby Book*, involves the seven Bs:

Birth bonding: A good experience in the first few hours after birth is regarded as very important for establishing secure attachment.

Belief in the signal value of your baby's cries: Parents are taught to interpret their baby's cries and to respond quickly and appropriately to them.

Breastfeeding: This is believed to have physical and psychological advantages for both mother and child.

Babywearing: The term was first used by Dr Sears and it means carrying the baby in a sling or other carrier, close to the body of the caregiver at all times.

Bedding close to baby: Sleeping in the same room and preferably in the same bed as the baby is encouraged, as is frequent breastfeeding at night.

Balance and boundaries: Appropriate responsiveness in terms of knowing when to say yes and when to say no is necessary for a healthy family life.

Beware of baby trainers: Instead of taking advice about how to 'train' the baby to make it cry less and sleep for longer stretches, parents are encouraged to listen to their own instinct and intuition.[3]

---

3   Dr William Sears and Martha Sears, *The Baby Book: everything you need to know about your baby from birth to age two* (Little, Brown and Co., revised edition, 2003).

You might assume from what I have written in previous chapters that I wouldn't agree with many of these points. But this assumption would be incorrect. I feel very strongly that your baby and child's needs must be met – always. Creating and maintaining a close bond with your child can only be a good thing. It enables parents to get to know their little one in a very important and positive way. Take, for example, the second point above about crying. Dr Sears is not saying that you should never let your baby cry, but he is also not saying that you should always react. It is about reacting 'appropriately', but always with the best interests of your baby at heart.

As it is also important to know the difference between co-sleeping and bed-sharing, I'll briefly reiterate these key definitions from the discussion in chapter one. Co-sleeping involves a separate cot beside your bed that you place the baby back into once feeding is finished. Bed-sharing means that baby stays physically in your bed for the night and makes very little use of their cot. It is a personal choice, but as long as you are doing this safely, you shouldn't run into any difficulties, and everything will, for the most part be absolutely fine. Yet, whilst I would not be reprimanding anyone for doing so, bed-sharing is not something I would ever personally recommend as a long-term option.

And what about the final point Dr Sears makes, about being wary of baby trainers? Naturally I am going to defend my profession. Sears feels that many people, if they choose to go down the baby training route, will get so caught up in it that they lose the ability to read their babies' signals and cues. The technique that I recommend, and will go through with you step by step, is all about listening to your baby and how the child is crying. Being able to have a sense of what your baby needs at a given time allows parents to react to their little ones instinctively rather than prescriptively. It is not about changing your baby, it is more about changing your approach and tweaking some of the little one's schedules so that both you and baby will benefit.

So, while I agree that you should give some careful thought to the type of training you use, I genuinely don't feel that by engaging in coaching you will be doing your child any disservice. In fact, more often than not, everyone benefits. Of course you should be instinctive in your reactions to your own child, but I would always put extra emphasis on the importance of listening.

'Attachment parenting' has become a buzzword in the past few years. In my opinion, many parents – perhaps even most parents – practise an element of attachment parenting in their daily lives. Being an attachment parent is not about slavishly following all the rules exactly, but picking and choosing the elements that suit your baby, suit you and suit your family.

The choices you make for your family and how you raise your children are yours and only yours. It is really not anyone else's business. However, it is good to be aware of the outcomes to your decisions and it is prudent to check that no one is suffering or struggling as a result of your parenting decisions. The time may come when you feel a change needs to be made. Consulting someone outside the family if there are difficulties or stresses can often be very helpful. That is where guides like this one will help.

Is it ever too late to make a change?

It is definitely not too late to teach a child who is no longer a baby to learn positive sleep habits. Yes, it is easier to sleep train when children are still in their cot. However, the methods I advocate will work really well with older children as well.

Most children with poor sleep habits will eventually sleep through the night in their own rooms. However, for the most part things don't just get better by simply waiting for a phase to pass. Some phases can very quickly become habits, in my experience. Once sleep becomes a real problem for you and your family it is time to make changes. So, deal with things now, when the time is right, because the chances are that you'll have to deal with them eventually.

In general, once you have gone through a process of sleep training, the effects will last throughout your child's life. Of course, there may be events that cause sleep regressions – such as holiday times, starting crèche or school, or times of illness. The good news is that once a family has successfully sleep trained a child, both the parents and the child will then have the skills and confidence to get past a sleep regression and get back on track. It will usually take only one night of retraining to get a child's sleep back to where it was before the sleep regression.

In my opinion, gentle sleep-training techniques are beneficial for your child as you will be encouraging the development of a new skill. Alongside an ever-present need for patience, to sleep train your baby you will also need determination, consistency, a capacity for giving clear messages and the courage of your convictions to follow through even when your baby 'pulls on your heart strings'. Once started, it is definitely best to keep going.

Consistency and clear messages

Giving mixed messages is not an option. You must decide on a plan and stay with it over a reasonable period of time. I repeat: you do not want to confuse your baby.

Courage of your convictions

You must believe you are making a change for the right reasons. With love in your heart and patience at the ready you can feel secure in the correctness of your decision. Even just a little niggling doubt can make it difficult to follow through with sleep training.

As parents, you have a behavioural history with your baby and your child will know which buttons to press. Even from as young as four months old, your baby will begin to pre-empt what you are going to do next. When you start training, your baby will probably respond by being a bit cross, because you are now changing the way you used to meet the little one's expectations of you. This is completely normal and can be hard for your baby to accept initially; I promise you, however, that your baby will forget 'the old ways' very quickly. This I have learned from experience.

Determination

Determination is key to your role when you decide to make a change. You must be determined enough to follow through with any adjustments once you have started.

Breastfeeding and sleep coaching

In my experience, difficulties can arise with attempting some sleep coaching when mums have opted to exclusively breastfeed their baby. I do not intend to get into the great breastfeeding versus formula-feeding debate because, as far as I am concerned, it is a hugely personal choice. We are regularly informed about the benefits of breastfeeding for both mum and baby. It is every parent's personal choice and I am unwilling to stand in judgement on one parent's choice over another. I feel exactly the same way about sleep coaching, by the way. It, too, is a very personal decision and, I believe, though beneficial, it is not for everyone. I am an 'each to their own' kind of person and have great respect for all lifestyle choices.

Many people would suggest that breastfed babies become dependent on the breast and, by extension, their mother, and that's why they don't sleep well at night. I can assure you that there are just as many babies who are utterly dependent on bottles of formula milk to get to sleep, so I would advise parents to have confidence in their decisions.

I also don't want anyone to feel that breastfeeding and a good night's sleep are mutually exclusive. They are not. It is absolutely possible to have both. With breastfeeding, it can just be a little more challenging. Formula-fed babies are more likely to stretch for longer periods without feeds, but there are lots of breastfed babies who can do it too – so you can have a great sleeper who is exclusively breastfed. Difficulties arise when little ones start to rely on the breast as their comfort method, rather than just for feeding, particularly at night. There is no exact way of telling at what age your baby will stop needing a feed during the night – each baby is different and it can simply depend on how fast they digest food. Breast milk is generally much more easily digested than formula, so breastfed babies may need feeding more regularly.

A breastfed baby will sometimes wake out of habit and at other times wake from hunger. Often mum and baby are quite in tune with each other and can feed with very little disruption overnight. But it can be hard to distinguish between hunger and habit, needs and wants. Confusion is caused when you debate with yourself whether to feed or to try to resettle without one. The best thing to do is trust your instincts, decide on a cause for waking and respond to it.

If you are still breastfeeding regularly overnight and feel that you have possibly become a 'human soother' to some extent, you could consider night weaning – but only if it feels right for you. It is definitely worth bearing in mind that your baby may be getting more comfort from you than sustenance during these feeds, and it might be worth considering sleep training and eliminating these overnight 'feeds'.

Getting organised to begin coaching

There are several things you might want to have organised, or at least on standby, if you are considering sleep training your baby.

It is a good idea, if your little one is a 'soother baby', to have a few soothers in your pocket at the ready. Many babies will think it is a great idea to throw the soother out of the cot for you to retrieve. There is nothing more entertaining for them than to see you scrambling on all fours around their bedroom floor picking up stray soothers! This will be a bit of a game for them, and we certainly do not want to allow playtime in the wee small hours of the morning. Having several soothers at the ready will spare you this.

Remove or at least put away any toys and books you may have stored in the baby's bedroom in the hope of keeping your child entertained in the middle of the night. Remove all toys and mobiles from the cot. They can simply end up being little more than a distraction to the job in hand – which is, of course, sleep. You cannot expect your baby to settle down in an overstimulated environment. 'Bells and whistles' in the cot may be provided with the best of intentions, but they are almost always counterproductive to sleep!

Toys can also serve as 'weapons', which older babies can use to throw out of the cot (as described regarding soothers above) to create distraction and grab your attention!

It is handy to have spare bedclothes – sheets, pyjamas, gro-bag, etc. – at the ready in case of leaky nappies or vomiting. I don't want to linger too much on the vomiting point, as I would rather that you didn't worry that your baby might get so wound up he or she would vomit. It is definitely not the norm, but it can occasionally happen. When we go through the techniques later, you will understand that my intention is that little ones never get to a point when they are completely overanxious or distressed, therefore avoiding the possibility.

You could perhaps give your baby one comfort toy to keep in the cot – something that will remind your child that it's bedtime. Such toys are not essential, but many babies and parents do favour them. Should your little one not have a particular affection for a comfort item, then don't worry about that. Many children do without them, although I think that nowadays, for whatever reason, they are more likely to have them. (By the way, if there is one particular item that your little one loves, buy a few of them. These items can get lost or damaged pretty easily, and it might be a good idea to stock up if you can afford them. But whatever you choose, make sure it is safe and doesn't have buttons or eyes or too many strings that could hurt or choke your baby.)

Soothers

Many of the families that I meet tell me that their little ones use a soother, and will mention it in an almost apologetic tone. I am *not* anti-soother, particularly as they come recommended by NICE. But, if your baby doesn't already use one, I wouldn't start introducing them at a later age. In any case, trying to introduce a soother to an older baby may be a wasted effort, as more than likely they won't take it.

I am, in fact, a fan of soothers, as they can be incredibly helpful for settling your baby's breathing into a natural and calm rhythm. They may often provide a good solution for some sleep issues; and yet, paradoxically, they can come with their own problems (for example the 'throwing-out-of-the-cot' scenario described previously).

If children are waking up at night looking for their soother, but settle back quickly once it is found, I generally don't think that sleep training will be the answer. These are what I simply describe as 'soother runs' and, while still disruptive to your sleep, they are a minimal disruption for your child. I wouldn't expect babies to be able to retrieve soothers by themselves until they are roughly eight months of age. For babies of eight months plus, I often feel the need to comment on a fabulous product called the Sleepytot Bunny. It is genuinely one of the only things I recommend to parents in terms of sleep gimmicks and gadgets.

This bunny is flat, like a cloth, but it has four paws to which you attach a soother, using little Velcro straps. I know that some soothers – such as those by MAM – don't have the little looped handles, but you can get a little attachment for these. The bunny doubles up as a comfort toy; over time, your little one will be able to rummage around in the cot and find the bunny, knowing that there are four soothers available!

A cheaper alternative would be to take a soft breathable piece of fabric and stitch some Velcro onto it yourself on which to attach soothers. Get creative!

Many people will decide simply to scatter a few soothers around the cot.

As long as you feel soothers aren't creating any problems, then I certainly have no issue with them.

Sleep coaching and twins

Sleep coaching can be complex enough with one child, so it naturally has greater complexity with twins and multiples. Even though there will be two, three, or even more babies, there will still be only one of you!

Generally, if one twin is more disrupted in terms of sleep than the other, and the twins are currently sharing a room, I would advise parents to move the 'rowdy' twin out to create an opportunity to sort out the sleep issue. When this is not possible, I generally explore other options with the parents. One suggestion might be to move the good sleeper in with one parent, or both, for a few nights while the parents tackle a little sleep coaching with their poor sleeper.

Where this is not possible, I suggest that parents place the good sleeper furthest from the door, even if they are relatively unfazed by their twin's wailing, so the good sleeper may be a little less disrupted by a parent entering and leaving the room. Chances are your good sleeper is more bothered by your movements than by their crying twin.

If both twins are poor sleepers, I usually recommend that their parents proceed with some sleep training and I advocate the introduction of new skills to both babies at the same time. This sounds exhausting, I know, but it will be worth it in the long run.

Having read this far it is hoped that you would be armed with a plan to tackle general bedtime/naptime with young babies, whether single babies or multiples.

Quite often, simply having a little more structure during the day will have a knock-on effect at night-time. But what if simply changing their daytime routine doesn't seem to be enough. What happens next? The answer could well be the sleep coaching route, which I will now go on to explain.

5

SLEEP COACHING
TECHNIQUE IN THE COT

The worst thing in the world is to try to sleep and not to.

F. Scott Fitzgerald

Various sleep coaching methods

So, by now you will have enough information to know if sleep coaching is an avenue you would like to explore. From my research, there is no real evidence that any one type of training works better than another, so whatever you decide to do, as long as you stick to it and give it some commitment, you will see great results.

My technique is based not only on my educational training and my fifteen years' experience of looking after babies, but it has also been reinforced by the hundreds of families I have helped. It combines elements of other methods in a way that I feel teaches babies to fall asleep and resettle themselves on their own, with the comfort of having a parent nearby.

There are of course many different techniques to choose from, apart from mine. They are pretty badly named in my opinion, as they are called 'extinction methods' – not exactly conjuring up images of kind, gentle, supportive coaching or guidance! Nonetheless, I will outline the main ones as, no doubt, you will come across them and it can be helpful to understand exactly what the various names signify.

Total extinction methods

There are two total extinction methods.

Controlled crying – no checking (sometimes called 'Cry it out')

This involves bringing baby up to the cot after your normal bedtime routine, saying goodnight and leaving. You do not go back in to check on baby. You do not offer any comfort or reassurance. You simply let the little one sort himself or herself out.

You place the baby in the cot. Walk out. Close the door. And that's it. You don't go back in until morning (or, during naps), until it is time to get up.

Controlled crying with checking

This is not dissimilar to the above method except that you will go in to the baby, but simply to check that the little one has not become stuck in the cot-rails, or has not been sick. You simply re-adjust the baby, re-dress him or her if necessary, and leave again.

Lots of people feel that the total extinction methods are the only way to teach little ones to sleep well at night. They might say things like, 'Three nights and we never looked back,' or, 'Tough love is the only thing that worked for us.' Neither of these methods appeal to me. I am *not* a fan. Although you aren't confusing children by going to them when they cry and thus reinforcing a 'cry and we will come back' type behaviour, in my opinion it is somewhat cruel and unnecessary. Please don't do it.

Total extinction methods are very harsh. They are not in the least supportive, and I do not suggest these to anybody undertaking sleep training. Your child will only learn that you will not come back to them when they need you. This is not a great starting point for any budding relationship. In theory these methods may work faster than others, but the results may be short-lived. Having a more gradual approach will mean that the message will become more familiar to your baby and a gentler learning experience will happen.

Gradual extinction methods

There are five gradual extinction methods.

Controlled comforting

This is a little like controlled crying as it involves leaving your baby to cry for either a set period of time, or for extended periods of time, before you go in and reassure/comfort the little one. You might decide to put your baby into the cot, say goodnight and walk out of the room. You might leave him or her to try to settle for a few minutes. Go back in after two minutes to reassure the little one. Then go in after four minutes to offer reassurance, then after six minutes and so on. This may or may not involve picking the baby up to comfort him or her. This type of coaching is more commonly known as 'Ferberising', as it is a technique that was created by Dr Richard Ferber of Boston Children's Hospital.

Elastic band technique

This is very similar to the controlled comforting method, but you do not increase the amount of time before you go to your little one. The other difference is that you do not leave the room. You do not hide in the dark though; you continue to move around the room, going so far as the door but always coming back to your baby after five minutes. It's as if you have an elastic band attached to the door, and you are pulling it taut when you go to your child, but releasing as you move away from your child. Your baby will know you are there.

For example, you decide to go to the little one and offer reassurance every five minutes. No more, no less. But you remain always in your baby's room throughout the process.

Note: The duration is optional. A parent decides on a time and sticks to it. The technique doesn't prescribe a five-minute window, but I personally would not recommend any longer than that.

Pick up–put down

This method is one of the more common sleep techniques used. To elaborate: Place your child in the cot. When the baby cries, go to the little one, pick him or her up for a cuddle and reassurance, then put them back down. Should the little one cry again, you immediately pick them up again, reassure them and place them back in the cot. This continues until your baby doesn't cry any more once placed back in the cot.

Chances are you won't get an opportunity to leave the room between pick-ups. This can be time consuming and it's easy to lose patience, but if you stick to your guns it can be a very effective technique. This technique is often recommended for use with newborns, but – as you already know – I am not a supporter of any kind of full-on training with very young babies.

Later in this book, you will see that the techniques that I find work best for my clients include a combination of the above. And although it seems like a mash-up of methods, it is very effective, because, I believe, consistency is always a common thread and there is an element of 'sameness'.

The following two techniques are normally used for an older child who repeatedly gets out of bed.

Door closing

This technique was also made popular by Dr Ferber and is usually used when children are big enough to climb over a gate that they have in their door frame. Bring your child to his or her room. Leave and close the door. You are asked to forcibly hold the door closed for a number of minutes before opening it again, bringing the child back to bed and leaving again. Hold the door closed firmly. You may speak to your child through the door, offering some words of comfort and to let the little one know that you are there, but do not have full-on conversations with your child. When you open the door again, you do not bring the child back to bed and offer nothing but a simple word or two of encouragement, then return to your post outside the door, holding it closed.

Rapid return

Again, this is used for older children continuously getting out of bed or leaving their rooms. And it is exactly as you might suspect – bringing your toddler back to bed in silence quickly and gently and, with as little fuss as possible, putting him or her back into bed. This is a little like 'pick up–put down' for the younger babies, in that it is boring and repetitive for you, but it can yield great results. It is a technique I would regularly use with toddlers. You are teaching the child the same 'lesson', and while the process I use is slightly different, the end result is the same.

My own technique

We are now getting to the satisfying part! I will show you how to settle your child at bedtime, and also to settle him or her later in the night when he or she wakes up.

This technique is based on my experiences as a sleep coach. Should you wish to investigate, there is plenty of documentation available in support of this approach. In my experience, the pros outweigh the cons, and the bottom line is this: it works! There will be tears, but they will be short-lived and not as a result of parents ignoring their child's needs.

It's a case of a little short-term pain for long-term gain, so to speak. Things may sometimes feel as though they get a little worse before they get better, but I can assure you, in line with my practice and experience, it is all progress.

My technique for settling a baby from six months

My technique is a four-step programme, with the fourth step repeated until your little one falls asleep.

Ensure that you are prepared for training by having the following in place:

- Your baby is in his or her *own room* for the entire night.

- The room is dark, with no night light.

- Toys are taken from the cot.

- Soothers are at the ready (if you use them).

Night schedule

6.00 p.m.	**Start winding down for the evening**
7.00/7.15 p.m.	**Milk feed and bedtime**

At bedtime, bring the baby to the cot and put them down awake or drowsy – but aware of where he or she is. Say, 'Night night, Sweetheart. I love you', and *leave* the room. (Note: You can replace 'Night night, Sweetheart. I love you' here and throughout with whatever 'tag line' you want to use: something you say every night to your child, which becomes a strong sleep association.)

Step one

Listen outside the door, and when you think your baby may be about to rev up (cry/shout at a higher pitch) go in to reassure him or her. Pick your baby up and whisper, 'Sshhhh. Night night, Sweetheart. I love you.' Soothe your baby and wait for the little one to calm down. Once baby is calmed, but not yet asleep, place baby back in the cot and *leave*.

This first reassurance may take only a few moments, as inevitably your baby will be quite happy to see you and is probably waiting for you to do all the things you did previously.

Listen outside the door.

Step two

When you think your baby is about to rev up again, go in and pick the little one up again. Whisper, 'Sshhhhh. Night, night Sweetheart. I love you.' Soothe baby and wait for him or her to calm down. Place baby back in the cot. *Leave.*

Listen outside the door.

Step three

The third time you go in after listening carefully to your baby, and when you feel that your little one needs you, re-enter the room and pick baby up.

This time, you will do so *in silence*. This is the beginning of mum and dad reducing their communication with their child so that the child is beginning to get a little less from you. Hold your baby and wait for him or her to calm down. If you previously rocked your baby until they fell asleep, you may want to try to avoid doing this from now on. Simply hold your baby. You will instinctively move while you are doing this, but try not to rock the little one. (In saying that, if the rocking provides some comfort, then gently do so. Remember though, that you are doing so only until your baby has calmed down sufficiently to place him or her back in the cot, not until baby is asleep.) When baby is calm, place him or her back in the cot and *leave.*

Listen outside the door.

Step four

When you think your little one is about to rev up, go in. Simply go to your baby in the cot and place your hand on baby's chest/back and wait for him or her to calm. Again, this is a further step into reducing what your baby gets from you when you go in.

From now, you will no longer be picking up and reassuring

your baby. You simply reassure the little one by touch alone. Once baby has calmed down, but not fallen asleep, *leave*.

Continue with this process until baby falls asleep.

Notes on the steps given above

You may ask how long you should wait with your child before leaving? The answer is, until your child is calm, no matter how long that takes.

And what if your child really doesn't seem to be calming down? Your baby may calm down quite quickly during the first three steps where you have picked them up, as the little one is delighted to see you again. But quite often, the further into the process you go, the less likely your child is to calm down. Baby will start to realise that you are doing something different and, most likely, will not be overly impressed.

Often, if babies are showing no signs of calming, it is because they don't like what you are doing or they don't want what you are offering. But: this is all you are offering. If they are not calming down, it may be an idea to put baby down and walk away, even just for a moment. Chances are, by holding back a little, the little one will be more likely to accept your new comfort method when you return.

Some parents have told me that they really felt that by picking their baby up 'one more time', they would be able to get a level of calm back into the situation. If your gut instinct tells you that one more pick-up might help, then do it, by all means. Just not repeatedly.

When you are out of the room and your child is upset (and not just angry with you or 'shouting'), you are to go in and reassure them – no matter how many times that means. This is not about waiting to see if your baby will stop crying after a while. If you feel that you need to go to your baby and, more importantly, that your baby needs you, you are not to wait.

There are only two occasions where I accept persistent crying and where it is all right to leave your baby crying in the cot for a short period. Remember, your child is safe and is protesting against the new arrangement. The little one will be absolutely fine for a few moments. The two occasions are these:

1. Should your baby be 'fighting' with you by pushing your hands away from him or her: I recommend that you do not put up resistance, but that you simply *leave*. If baby is fighting you, then he or she does not want what you are offering. From mum and dad's point of view, you are not willing to offer anything else. So, leaving is the best option – even if it is only to walk out of the door and immediately come back in again. It may be that baby accepts what is being offered at that later stage. Leaving also gives you an opportunity to catch your own breath and clear your head, or perhaps grab a glass of water or brush your teeth. Your baby is safe. Regroup, refocus and get back to the job in hand.

2. If mum wants dad to take over from her and vice versa: If you need back-up, go and get it. Don't wait for someone to take over from you. Ask your partner to help and remind your partner to resume from where you left off. (This four-step process can be a little bit stressful for parents, particularly if they are on their own, so if you'd like to, perhaps invite a friend or family member to stay with you while you go through this period of change.)

What happens when baby wakes later during the night?

Exactly the same process is used for both going to bed and for further wake-ups. Should your baby wake up an hour or less after he or she finally falls asleep, start from where you left off, as baby has only really done one or two sleep cycles.

Should your baby sleep for an extended period (more than a couple of hours) without waking, then I recommend that you start from the beginning again, as this is a new phase of sleep.

Cot training: what to expect

The idea of this section is to let you know the sort of things that may happen when you start training little ones to sleep in their cots for the entire night – just so you know what you might face. I also suggest you don't underestimate these little people. Perhaps all along they have been waiting for a few boundaries. They do like them, you know! Each case is different, but as the nights go by you will start to see great changes occurring before your eyes.

If you have been allowing your little one to fall asleep – be it from rocking or on the bottles/feeds – before you place him or her in the cot, one of three things will happen that first time when you put your baby down while still alert:

- Baby will be so surprised, that he or she just rolls over and falls asleep.

- Baby will remain quiet for a number of minutes (even up to twenty minutes or so) and then will decide that this is not what he or she wants, and will begin to let you know.

- Baby will immediately rev up and show you what he or she is thinking!

You may have to go in to your baby straightaway if he or she is upset, or you may be able to wait a while before things start to get going and the crying starts. When you pick the little one up the first time, baby will calm down fairly quickly as he or she will be delighted and think that you have changed your mind. The next couple of times, it may take your baby longer to settle, as baby is now beginning to get a little wary of your proposed new settling ideas, and doesn't know what to expect from you next.

Once you move on to step four, where you are only placing your hand on your baby's chest or back, things can get a little more difficult, as it can take longer to settle babies this way. Stick with it. If you need to take a breather, do so. Ask your partner to come and take over.

If your baby has soothers, he or she may start throwing them out of the cot. Have a stash of soothers at the ready – you don't want to spend any time fumbling in the dark. This won't happen with your six-month-old, but as your child gets older it is more likely. Perhaps invest in the Sleepytot Bunny as mentioned before!

An older baby may start to realise quite quickly that things have changed and, rather than be upset, may decide to play for a while. That is fine. Leave them be.

Remember, you are going in only if your baby is distressed and needs you. Older babies may also simply get bored by the palaver. Some might take their clothes off or get out of their gro-bags. Leave them be. You can re-dress them swiftly once they fall asleep!

You may feel that if you picked your baby up some time after completing those first three steps, the little one would calm more easily for you. Please do not go against your instincts, but remember that what we are trying to do is slowly reduce the level of contact and communication with these little ones, so that each time they get a little less from you when you are present with them.

You might find that your baby gets a little annoyed or frustrated when you have your partner come in to settle him or her. Try to stick with it, but don't aggravate your baby too much. It's not fair. Baby may not be used to the other partner settling him or her, particularly if baby is normally breastfed to sleep. I simply want you both to have an idea of the technique to use.

Breath holding and vomiting – which may or may not happen, but occasionally do – can be scary. I would suggest that if they do, you have waited too long before going in to your baby, and the little one is feeling insecure and things have gone a little too far. Be careful. You have to really tune in to your baby. Familiarise yourself with baby's cries. If breath holding or vomiting has happened, please take your baby out of the cot. Clean baby up if necessary and, as always, offer some comfort. Then, start from the beginning again.

As time goes on, you will see gradual progress as your little one gets used to this new regime. Things may be getting progressively better as the nights go by, but then, all of a sudden, one night may come when it feels as though they have taken a nosedive. This is what is known as a 'kick-back night'; although it is uncommon, it can occur. When I meet parents who say they tried a sleep-coaching method for a few days and then it stopped working, it is likely they are referring to the kick-back night. It would normally happen after three to four nights of training, but can happen even up to a week to ten days after training begins. Just be aware of it. Put your game-faces back on and get through it. Try not to go back to the old ways.

It is important to be mindful of your relationship with your partner if you are undergoing any sort of training with your little one. Although you are both singing from the same song sheet in terms of the outcome you hope for, it can be very easy for one parent (and sorry, mums, it's usually you) to assume that the other is 'probably not doing it right'! Mum may want to go in all guns blazing and take over from dad, when in fact he is doing just fine. This is unfair to him. He wants the same thing and he knows the plan. Leave him to it, unless he asks for help. It is a kick in the teeth for one partner to feel undermined by the other. Just be careful of each other's feelings!

Case study: bedtime angel, midnight devil

I received a phone call one evening from a mum of two, who was expecting her third child at the time. Her youngest child, Martha, had suffered greatly with reflux from birth and, as a result, her sleeping patterns and the manner in which she settled were all over the place. Because a new baby was on the way, her parents were keen to get some sort of shape on Martha's daytime and night-time patterns as soon as possible. At this point, Martha was eight months old and was being bottle fed. She was also taking three solid meals a day.

It was my feeling – and in hindsight it proved to be correct – that we should wait until mum was able to get Martha's medical issues under control. At the time, her paediatrician had recommended one of the 'comfort' milk formulas for Martha, but it was increasingly difficult to find it. In the end, by changing the formula, in conjunction with offering a prescribed medication for the reflux, the health issue subsided.

Because Martha had an older brother who needed dropping off and collecting from various activities, her parents were finding it difficult to keep a structure in her day. She would nod off in the back of the car or, more often than not, in the buggy. But at bedtime this little girl would go down to her cot with very little fuss and was happy enough to be in her cot and fall asleep by herself. Martha was still unable to pull herself up to standing in the cot and she slept in her own room every night.

However, later at night, anything might happen. On average, Martha would wake up to three times a night – sometimes more, sometimes less. When she woke, a number of things could occur. Dad might go in and push down on the mattress to give her a bit of motion in the hope that she would nod off. This sometimes worked. Sometimes her parents would rock her back to sleep. Sometimes they would turn music on, and sometimes they would turn it off. Or Martha might fall asleep on mum's lap, almost lying across her knees. Occasionally, and as a last resort, they might offer her a bottle. Sometimes a combination of these things worked, but nothing in particular consistently helped Martha to get back to sleep again.

Her parents were also concerned about her waking her older brother, who was in pre-school and needed his sleep. Mum and dad needed theirs too! Both parents attended to Martha when she woke – with mum doing most of the settling midweek and dad in a position to help out more at the weekends.

We discussed a plan of action, taking into account the need for a better daytime structure so that Martha was not overtired going to bed.

For her daytime, we decided upon the following routine for Martha at nine to ten months:

7.00/7.30 a.m.	Wake and bottle
8.30 a.m.	Breakfast

(Maybe a short sleep around 9.30 a.m. but wake at 10 a.m.)

10.30 a.m.	Snack and water
11.45 a.m.	Dinner/lunch
12.30 p.m.	*Sleep* (up to two hours)
2.30/3.00 p.m.	Bottle/feed – 7 fluid ounces (210 millilitres)
4.00 p.m.	Snack

(May have a short twenty-minute nap at 4.30 p.m.)

5.30 p.m.	Tea
6.45 p.m.	Wind-down time for everyone
7.30 p.m.	Bottle and *bed*

This suited Martha's mum as her son needed collecting at midday from a local pre-school, and it allowed them to have some quiet time together while Martha slept. He was being dropped off by car in the morning, so we felt that it wasn't the end of the world if Martha had her morning nap en route. I also reassured them that if Martha were to skip the late afternoon nap, which many children do at this age, then they should try to get her down to bed a little earlier. Even twenty minutes earlier would start to make a difference.

I explained to Martha's mum that, quite often, it is harder to sleep coach at night when the little ones initially go down to bed quite well. This is mainly because it doesn't give the parents an opportunity to get used to going through the steps when they aren't so tired themselves. It can be good to have a dry run, so to speak. But Martha's mum and dad were determined to give it their best shot; by the time I left, I too was confident that they would stick with it.

I had also explained that it was likely on that first night that Martha would not necessarily 'learn' how to get back to sleep unaided, and that she would probably sleep only as a result of being exhausted. I pointed out that mum and dad would be learning the most out of the three of them that first night. However, I reminded them that Martha would become familiar with this new expectation and would come to know that bottles, rocking and music, etc., were no longer going to be part of the night-time experience.

We decided to take a few days to adjust to the new daytime routine, and then to tackle the nights.

The changes in daytime went really well; after a few days Martha's mum rang me to let me know that they were going to go ahead that night. By the time the night-time training actually started, Martha had already made great strides towards learning to settle herself. The awakenings were less frequent, and her daytime sleep was going really well. With a few words of encouragement, I awaited their updates.

Within three weeks of our chat, Martha had slept every night except one, when her sleep was disrupted due to teething. Her mum and dad were thrilled. Four months later, with everyone rested and recovered, Martha and her family welcomed a baby sister.

Sleep coaching when your child can stand up in the cot

The main difference here is that your older baby or toddler, while still in a cot, is much more clued in to the changes going on around him or her. At this stage, older babies or toddlers are much more aware of their surroundings. They are also more physically competent. They may already be standing up in the cot when you go in.

You will still be maintaining the same technique as for younger babies, but it can feel like the battle is a little bit harder. On a positive note, in my experience these little ones usually accept the new regime relatively fast, as they are quite quick to pick up new skills.

Problems arise because these little ones are like yo-yos, regularly bouncing up and down from standing to sitting to lying. They can be relentless! You have the additional difficulty now in calming their physical activity as well as any emotional displays.

My advice would be simply to put older babies or toddlers back lying down each time you go to them. As you are staying with them until they are calming down, you may end up placing them back down on the mattress a number of times each time you are comforting them. But, if they are standing up and really having a hard time settling down, then I suggest that rather than removing them from the cot, you simply comfort them while they are standing. Rest your child's little head on your chest while he or she is standing, and comfort and console the little one in this position until he or she calms down again.

Case study: the all-night bottle guzzler

Susie was a nineteen-month-old toddler and the youngest of three children. When her mum contacted me, she was expecting baby number four. Like Martha, Susie went down fairly easily most nights, occasionally kicking off a bit. Her parents gave her a bottle once she was in her sleeping bag and then put her to bed, where she finished it off, with a top-up if she didn't immediately settle.

She usually woke at least twice after that. Her parents tried giving her water or a soother, but inevitably caved in and gave her a bottle of milk.

Susie's daytime routine also had a part to play in the night-time antics. Her mum had to pick up her sister at 12.50 p.m. and her brother at 2.20 p.m., so Susie was in and out of the car or buggy until 3 p.m. She usually took a nap in her cot at 3 p.m. for an hour and a half. She settled for the nap easily once she had a bottle. The problem here was that this big nap was really too late in the day for Susie.

Susie was a great eater and had lunch around 12.30 p.m., tea at 5 p.m. and a snack before bed.

In chapter three you will have seen my suggested routine for children older than twelve months. Susie was a good example of how specific routines don't work for everyone and sometimes need to be adjusted. This routine didn't quite fit with Susie's family life so we changed it a little. If you are too focused on times and locations, you will lose the ability to adapt your day to your circumstances. This will cause frustration and you may eventually give up, whereas, in fact, a little bit of flexibility and tweaking is all that's required.

We adjusted the routine to ensure that Susie was getting enough sleep during the day and also that her sleep was at appropriate times. As it was, she mainly nodded off briefly on school runs, which wasn't ideal, and then had that large nap later in the day at around 3 p.m. I felt that this resulted in Susie not being ready for bed at 7 p.m. – she had napped too late in the day to be tired enough by then.

But napping wasn't the only issue here for Susie. Her dependence on her bottles to fall asleep was a huge problem, not to mention the amount of milk this family would go through in a day! Susie's parents knew that she did not need this extra milk and had tried not giving it to her. They gave in, however, when she started screaming. Susie was the right weight for her age and was generally a very healthy toddler.

Options for helping Susie

These were the two options we discussed for helping Susie during the night:

1. Going cold turkey: If/when Susie wakes, do not offer her a bottle. Her parents knew that she had had sufficient food and fluids during the day. Susie associated the bottle with settling herself back to sleep and didn't know how to sleep without it.

   Advantage: Quick and effective and saves a fortune on milk!

Disadvantage: May take a few nights for her to realise milk/bottle is not forthcoming.

2. Reduce the amount of milk Susie gets during the night by a couple of ounces each time, so that eventually she will be getting so little that it becomes insignificant for her.

    Advantage: Still allowing Susie to think she is getting what she wants, but the parent is in control and is slowly taking control back from Susie.

    Disadvantage: May take a little longer, but the end result is the same: no more bottles!

We went for option 1! Together, we decided to cut the bottles out during the day by going 'cold turkey'. It was also important that Susie went to bed at night having drunk her bottle downstairs, and that she went into the cot awake – giving her an opportunity to self-soothe and losing the association with the bottle as being the only way she would go to sleep or go back to sleep.

When parents are eliminating feeds at night, it can take a few nights for children to realise a bottle is not forthcoming. But usually by the third night they will have forgotten all about it as their preferred way of falling asleep again. Remember, babies don't always wake for a specific reason. It is a natural part of their sleep cycles to rouse briefly at various stages through the night. More often than not, if they are unable to get back to sleep, it is because they are used to parents doing something to help them, as they have yet to master the skills to get back to sleep themselves.

I advised Susie's parents to keep records of the progress. They kept a daytime diary, including details of feeds (solids and bottles) and times of feeds. Through this diary we were able to see that the less she was drinking during the night, the hungrier she was during the day, and her daytime eating habits improved further.

We used the same technique with Susie as we had done with Martha. The only difference was that, although Susie was a little bit older and still in her cot (but showing no signs of climbing out), she was able to stand up by herself. We made a plan for this.

If she was standing up when her parents went in to her, they were to place her back lying down and stay with her until she calmed down. But if she was standing up and was very upset – only if she was having a 'complete meltdown' – they were to leave her standing, rubbing her back until she was nearly calm, and then place her back lying down in the cot.

I had also suggested to her parents that they arm themselves with soothers in case she reacted by throwing them at mum and dad.

If Susie woke during the night, her parents were to use the same process. I reminded them that should Susie then wake up an hour or less after her last arousal, they were to start from where they left off, as she had only really done one or two sleep cycles. If she went for an extended period without waking, then they were to start from the beginning again, as this is a new phase of sleep.

So how did it go?

On the first night, Susie took an hour to settle. That day, she had napped from 2 to 3 p.m., which was not ideal but a much better time for her to sleep than later in the day. Her mum was determined, and felt that bedtime went better than she expected. She was delighted that Susie nodded off eventually without the bottle. Susie woke later that night, but her mum and dad stayed strong and used their technique, and she went back to sleep till the morning.

On the second night, she took only ten minutes to fall asleep, and woke very briefly later on. Her mum and dad did not have to go past the third step with her, and she slept till morning.

On night three, Susie slept through the night without rousing her parents. This has continued to this day!

Early risers

Perhaps you may not be aware of this, but early-morning awakenings have a lot to do with what happened the day before. Often, a catch-22 situation ensues: your child has a poor night's sleep and then sleeps badly during the day.

Early risers generally wake sometime between 4 a.m. and 5 a.m., as this is the time that their sleep cycle can shift during the night. Daylight in summertime can also be a factor in early rising, as earlier sunrises affect the light in the room. You'll know yourselves how hard it can be for you to sleep when it is bright outside. It is equally as difficult for babies, as their circadian rhythm (internal body-clock) is affected by daylight. The light itself doesn't wake them, but it is normal for them to rouse at this time of the day, as their body will tell them it is wake-up time. Then, because it's bright outside, they find it difficult to resettle. Another factor can be sleeping well overnight and feeling refreshed at this hour; if this is the case, children will be less inclined even to attempt to go back to sleep.

Also, if children are overtired when going to bed, they often wake at this time (around 5 a.m.), which can then lead to cortisol being released into their bloodstream, and this acts like adrenaline. This can prevent children from getting back to sleep and may give rise to early starts to the day. As these children are in a light sleep in the morning time, it does not take a whole lot to rouse them fully; therefore if they are overtired, they will find it difficult to settle as their brain is working to keep them awake. But once resettled they are likely to go back into a deep sleep after this light phase.

If you don't attempt to resettle them, you will find that your little one could lose out on two hours' sleep each night. That's one full night's sleep in a week! Of course, parents will also lose out.

We all get set on a time for going to bed. However, you will need to change the bedtime hour if your child is waking up at 5 a.m. Children under the age of three to four will need approximately eleven to twelve hours' sleep at night for their optimal growth and development. Therefore I strongly advise you to aim to have your babies and toddlers asleep by 7 p.m. (7.30 p.m. at the latest).

When your child wakes early in the morning, there may also be a certain amount of habit already at play here. But you will need to be consistent in your approach, otherwise your child will not really know what to expect. Your baby won't know whether or not you are going to pick him or her up. This can be confusing for your baby. You may need to prepare yourself for a week or two of mum and dad getting up at 5 a.m. and trying to resettle your child until it is time to start the day. Use the same technique as laid out before.

Keep the room as dark as possible, and don't expect miracles. Chances are, for the first few days, your little one won't go back to sleep despite your best efforts, but over time things will start to change.

It is up to you, as a family, to decide what time is good to start the day. Be reasonable about it. Expecting your child to sleep from 7 p.m. until after 8 a.m. is simply unrealistic. Decide what 'morning' is for you. I suggest some time between 6 and 7 a.m., particularly if you are all getting up to go to work and get to crèche.

Just don't be disappointed at the weekend when you want a lie-in. You can't have your cake and eat it too!

(Note: If you are doing some training with your baby and the little one starts sleeping really well overnight until around 5.30 or 6 a.m., I would not be 'fighting' with the baby at that point. Your child is possibly sleeping more than he or she ever has and the body clock is adjusting. Give baby time to settle into this new volume of sleep.)

6

TODDLERS, BIG BEDS AND TANTRUMS

A well-spent day brings happy sleep.

Leonardo da Vinci

Cot to bed

When it's time to move your toddler from his or her cot to a bed, you might find that the only person anxious about it is you! Many children transition easily to their new sleeping arrangements with just a few simple words of encouragement. If you, as parents, are feeling anxious, your little one may pick up on this, so it's best to treat it as just something really normal. Some children will put up some resistance as they feel parents are taking away something they find comfort in and creating a brand-new environment. But, like anything, once you decide to make the move, try to keep moving forwards.

Two reasons why you might move your child into a bed

1. The first and most important one would be if your little one becomes a highly skilled escape artist and can manage to

fling themselves over the bars and out of the cot, arriving in to you with pride in their new-found gymnastic abilities (while you have a minor heart attack)! While more often than not they manage this without injury, it's simply too dangerous to keep them in their cot. My own mum recalls my first escape. She was happily chatting on the phone downstairs while I supposedly napped. She saw me wander down the stairs and into the sitting room. She nearly passed out – primarily from shock, but also because it meant her few hours' peace in the afternoons were in jeopardy!

2. You may have a new arrival on the scene who needs to move out of the Moses basket or crib and into the cot in which your two- to three-year-old is languishing. If this is the case, aim to make the move at least six to eight weeks before the new arrival is born, allowing your little one to get used to their new set-up. You also don't want your older child to feel 'pushed out' by the new sibling. In saying this, use your instincts, and if you feel that your little one is just not ready to move yet, perhaps borrow another cot for the short term.

Generally, most children are bed-ready somewhere between two and three years of age. Some move sooner and some later, but generally by three years old a toddler bed is the most appropriate sleeping place for them. Some might say that first children will resist this move more strongly than their siblings and that subsequent children move more easily because they want to be 'big', just like their older brother or sister. In my experience, though, it simply depends on the child and his or her temperament or personality.

Tips for helping your child make the move from cot to bed

- Go shopping for a new bed or just new bedcovers; get your child involved and excited about the event by asking them to go shopping with you. But don't go on about it too much! Kids are quick to pick up on adults' anxieties and you could have a battle on your hands. If you are not confident about the move, they sense it.

- Just like some adults have a favourite pillow or duvet cover, children also 'like what they like', so don't remove your child's comforts completely.

- Do not surprise your child with a new bed and expect the little one to accept it. Prepare your child and let him or her talk freely about it, particularly if the child has some questions or fears.

- If possible, place the new bed in the space where the cot used to be, so that your child's surroundings do not change too much. In this way the little one will still have familiar points of reference in the room, which he or she is used to seeing from the cot.

Having safety measures in place

As with all things child-related, safety is key. As long as your child is sleeping safely, there is no real issue as to the type of bed the little one is in. So if you choose to have your child in an adult-sized single or double bed, you should also put some pillows or cushions on the floor beside your little one, so when the inevitable happens – we have all fallen out of our beds at some stage! – there is a cushion there to soften the blow. And make sure, where possible, that you align at least one side of the bed beside a wall, so you aren't increasing the risk!

Bed rails are also important. These allow the little ones to feel secure and, although in general they are of a softer material than the cot bars, they are sturdy enough to withstand a bit of active moving around. (My niece thought they meant that you weren't allowed to get out! Bonus!)

Technique for making the move

Allow an hour or so to wind down in the evenings. After tea, it might be an idea to run a bath (although I don't believe a bath *has* to be an integral part of bedtime routines). Get dressed for bed and have some quiet and calm time with your children in the evenings. Explain to your child again about bedtime and sleeping in his or her own new bed. But – as I mentioned when suggesting bedclothes shopping – don't go on about it, or your toddler will sense you mightn't be as confident as you appear. We all know what the result could be: mayhem!

At bedtime (usually 7.30 p.m.) have the little one's night-time drink and a little snack downstairs, and maybe read one or two stories (if that's part of your normal wind-down). Remember: try not to change too much at once. Keeping the status quo means that kids are less wary of new things. Then, bring your little one up to bed for a *final* story (not negotiable!). Place your toddler into the bed, read your book and say goodnight. (You can either climb onto the bed with your child or sit on a chair or on the floor beside the little one while you are reading.) Remember to use your chosen tag line here – perhaps something like, 'It's bedtime, Little One. I love you.' Then you simply walk away and leave the room. If you normally close your child's bedroom door, continue to do so. But, if you normally leave the door ajar and have a landing light on, you can still do so. Just make sure you don't stand casting your shadow or where your child can see you, as they may keep running out to get you. Perhaps step into another room to avoid being spotted.

Be aware that one of two things might happen:

1. Your toddler may turn over and fall asleep.
2. Your toddler may immediately kick off or start calling for you.

Remember that these techniques are mainly about *listening* to your child. At no stage do we want children to feel scared or abandoned in their rooms. If your little one is upset, you must react accordingly. Acknowledge, though, that there may be a behavioural side to this and, as with the little ones still in cots, I would be less likely to interact with toddlers if they are simply playing up.

Tips for toddler sleep

- Create a bedtime routine that can become the anchor of your day: dinner, wind-down, bath, story, bed – or a similar routine that works for you. This should be a calm, peaceful time that doesn't stimulate your child. The process will soon become familiar, allowing your toddler to recognise what's about to happen and to know that bedtime is approaching.

- Make a reward chart, something fun you can create together. Involving your child in the process, rather than just buying one or making it yourself, may help encourage cooperation at bedtime. Alternatively, buy some inexpensive toys, stickers and other toddler-friendly prizes – if your child stays in bed/stops playing up at bedtime/sleeps all night in his or her own bed, choosing a toy is the reward. If not, no toy.

- Make your child's bedroom somewhere comfortable and inviting for bedtime. Involve your little one when setting up a new bedroom and choosing a duvet and pillow set. It gives them a sense of responsibility in this new process. The bedroom should be just that: a bedroom. Keep all distractions, toys and other exciting things in another room or downstairs, and as much as possible keep the bedroom a calm environment. There's only one job to do here and that is to sleep!

- If monsters and things that go bump in the night are an issue, re-use an old 'squirty bottle' – help your child decorate it, then explain that you are putting 'magic' spray inside. Let your little one give a few sprays around the room at bedtime to remove the scary things.

- Make it clear to your toddler that *this* is his or her bed and *that* is your bed. You may have slipped into some unexpected bed-sharing, and if you've decided that the time has come to reclaim your bed, you will need to make sure boundaries are set from the start.

- Ensure your child understands that it's night-time, and what that means.

- Don't continue to talk about the changes and new rules – your child will sense your anxiety. Your toddler's job is to push boundaries and yours is to set them. When it comes time for bed, put your toddler down with minimum fuss, chatting and stimulation.

- As with most elements of parenting, it's important to be persistent and consistent. It may take some determination to pursue the routine and get to the 'finish line', but consistency is key.

- Work as a team with your partner so that everyone knows the plan and sticks to it. If your toddler's bedtime antics or middle-of-the-night wake-ups continue, take turns returning the little one to bed – try to avoid a good cop–bad cop situation.

My technique for toddler bedtime: step by step

Here is my technique for encouraging toddlers to go to sleep and stay in their own beds. At bedtime, bring your little one up to bed and read your final story. Say goodnight and leave the room.

Step one

On first kick off, and when you think your toddler is about to rev up, go in. Whisper, 'It's bedtime, Little One. I love you. Sshhhhh' (or whatever tag line you have chosen), soothe your child (in his or her bed), and allow the little one time to calm down. Stay with your child until they are calm enough for you to leave again.

Step two

The second time, and when you think your toddler is about to rev up, go in. As with the first time, whisper your tag line and soothe your child (in his or her bed) and allow the little one time to calm down. You will be waiting with your toddler until any crying subsides. Try not to get into any conversation. If you are feeling the need to say something to your child, then repeat your tag line. Then simply get up and leave the room.

Step three

Any time after that, you don't say a word. Simply go back into your child's room each time and comfort the little one without being verbal at all. This can be hard, as quite often a few 'sshhhhh' sounds might just slip out! It's not the end of the world. Just don't get manipulated into conversations or demands!

Continue the above process until they fall asleep.

Notes on the steps given above

To be honest, I am assuming that these resourceful toddlers will be getting out of bed each time (and not just shouting at you from the bed). Take your child back calmly by the hand and tuck the little one back in.

Your toddler will, more than likely, look for communication from you each time, but try not to fall into this trap. *Don't* get into it with your child – it's neither the time nor the place.

Your toddler shouldn't need anything else other than to go to sleep, having been fed, had a bedtime drink and opportunities at your wind-down to tell you anything you might have wanted to know about their day. 'I forgot to tell you …' is not to be allowed! One little one I recently worked with spent a few hours demanding various things from her parents. Once they heard 'I need ketchup' from the top of the stairs, they realised that their crafty toddler was just pushing it! Another proceeded to go through her entire nursery-rhyme collection in an attempt to attract her parents' attention. When they didn't go in (although they were falling around laughing at her outside the door), she ended up just lying down and going to sleep! What a crafty little bunny!

Your tone of voice is important during the steps where I suggest that you are communicating with your toddler – not raising your voice or shouting, but delivering your message nonetheless. When you are addressing your little one, your tone must be confident and matter of fact. When you put your toddler back to bed, try to keep the atmosphere quiet and calm. Your child is likely to be drowsy (particularly during middle-of-the-night episodes). If you engage in a conversation, it could further wake the little one.

Try to resist the urge to stay with your child until he or she is close to sleep, as it may upset the little one further when you eventually get up to leave. Stay long enough for your child to have calmed down, but leave *before* he or she has fallen asleep. It has been my experience that once you stay with little ones until they actually go to sleep, it is often the first thing they remember when they wake up. Last thing your toddler knew, you were lying there beside him or her, sitting on a chair nearby. Now, you're gone. This throws toddlers, and it can be unnerving and a little distressing.

The process outlined in the steps given above can take multiple times (yes – even as many as a hundred!), but once your toddler sees that you are not changing your approach or giving up, he or she will soon get the consistent message and will have grown tired of a one-sided argument. The first night may be hardest, although sometimes children get such a surprise at the new approach that they just go to sleep!

What happens when your toddler wakes later during the night?

The above technique is used for the bedtime settling, but I would also suggest and encourage it for any middle-of-the-night episodes too. It applies to both scenarios. In fact, by using it at bedtime you will ensure that your toddler will be a little more used to it when you continue to use it during the night. This strategy also gives parents an opportunity for a trial run at bedtime. Once you see that your child manages to fall asleep without you present, you will be more confident to use it later on when you are exhausted and half-asleep.

Most importantly, *listen* to your child and *respond at the appropriate time* (and *in an appropriate manner*). If your toddler is just shouting at you from their bed, I suggest that you don't react. The shouting is quite probably what I describe as 'just nonsense'. But, if your child is upset, I would definitely continue going in to the little one to console them, then leaving again. This is not about children crying themselves to sleep – it is about encouraging them and supporting them through a new process. They have the skills; it is simply giving them coaching and guidance.

So, if your toddler wakes up an hour or less after their last wake-up or arousal, start from where you left off. For example: bedtime started at 7.30 p.m., and your child falls asleep at 9 p.m., and then wakes and calls for you or gets out of bed at 10 p.m. Start using your technique right from where you left off (simply bringing them back to bed in silence). The reason I suggest this is that the little one has really only gone through one sleep cycle and this initial wake-up can be treated as still being part of bedtime.

Should your child sleep for an extended period (more than one or two sleep cycles) without waking, then you start from the beginning again – that is, by communicating with your toddler and using your bedtime tag line. This is a new phase of sleep and so the resettling needs to start again.

The problems really manifest in the middle of the night, when parents are exhausted and the easiest thing may seem to be to let your toddler come into bed with you or, indeed, to jump into your toddler's bed with him or her. If your child insists on getting into your bed and out of his or her bed, firmly take the little one back without much fussing and limited cuddles. In this way, toddlers become aware of what is expected of them. It can feel a little like you're banging your head against a brick wall, but your persistence will be worth it. If toddlers are getting out of bed frequently during the night – perhaps even several times an hour – it can be incredibly frustrating and tiring for parents, but eventually they will wear themselves out and get the message that the parents' bed is simply not an option any more. Persist and it will get better; it's a matter of breaking the cycle. They will learn that constantly getting out of bed is a fruitless effort.

Parents often ask me how many hours this can take, but it really is very hard to quantify. Generally, the process at the toddler's actual bedtime can be long and arduous, but later wake-ups can be easier to settle. Unfortunately, there is no definitive answer here, but it mightn't be unusual for a couple of hours to pass whilst going through the steps. (Get your hands on a heavy-duty carpet, as it will be well worn!) Each case is different.

Bed hopping during training should be avoided if at all possible, as you may merely be creating problems for the future. It means that any good work you put in at the start of the night will have been a bit of a wasted effort. Nobody will have learned anything. If you let your toddler in with you once, or indeed, you get in with them, it will be harder to say no the next time; so it's best to be firm and put the little one back to bed each time he or she gets out.

(I don't want to deny you those lovely weekend cuddles in bed, though! I have so many fond memories of us all being in our parents' bed on Saturday or Sunday mornings, just chatting and shooting the breeze. But, I never remember either my mum or dad being asleep at the time. If you are a fan of lazy weekend mornings, by all means scramble in together. Just don't do it for the sake of catching a few more minutes' sleep. We are trying to show toddlers that mum and dad's bed is not available to them for sleeping!)

By not getting involved with chats and various requests at night, you will help your toddler realise that it is a bit of a one-sided conversation and actually quite boring. So, a reminder: ignore the demands for water, the complaints of pains in various parts of the body and the need for particular teddies or comforts.

(As an aside, there is one time when I feel that maybe your toddler's demands should be heard – if you are potty training your little one and looking to toilet train at night-time. If your toddler says he or she needs to use the loo, this is a hard one to argue with, as nobody wants an unnecessary full change of clothes! Just ensure you have cut back on drinks before bedtime. It might be a good idea to lift your sleeping toddler and pop the little one on the loo before you go to bed. Give them the benefit of the doubt the first couple of times they ask to go to the loo. If there is no actual weeing each time, for a number of nights, chances are they're messing with you!)

There is an argument for taking the actual bedtime and the later wake-ups or disturbances as separate issues. But, in my opinion, why prolong something that you can sort out with less time and less disruption? Start as you mean to go on. Remember, we are trying not to give our children mixed signals. Clear messages are the order of the day.

On another, but related note, some people will decide that this is also a good time to get rid of the soother – part of growing up, so to speak. I would suggest that you make the transition first and then deal with the soother as a separate issue. Too much change is unnerving for little ones and you don't want to make the experience too traumatic. Ultimately, I want to be fair to them. Big beds are a big deal!

Bed training: what to expect

As was the case with my discussion of cot training (in chapter five), I think it's a good idea to outline here the types of things that may happen when you start training little ones to sleep in their beds, alone, for the entire night – just so you know what you might face. Each case is different, yet as the nights pass, great changes will happen! This list outlines the things that I have encountered from toddlers over the last few years during bed training:

- Consistently getting out of bed.

- Consistently coming downstairs.

- Staying in bed but shouting and/or kicking the walls.

- Refusing one parent and demanding another.

- Taking off their nappies and even their pyjamas (this is a current favourite of my god-daughter – her mum has to react as she doesn't want her to wet the bed or freeze!).

- Singing or performing nursery rhymes.

- Requesting anything from the expected (drinks or particular teddies) to the ridiculous (ketchup!).

Ask toddlers what they want and I have no doubt they will say 'everything'! (And probably only on *their* terms!) Part of your role as parents is to help put boundaries in place for your children. In saying that, they have a job to do too – and that is to test the limits you put in place for them. Without these boundaries, you are not doing your job. Setting limits as to what is acceptable behaviour at bedtime will stand to you in the long run.

As you will have read over and over again in this book, *listen* to your child. Identify those times when your child is in need or, alternatively, when your little one is simply 'trying it on'! You are the adult and you need to be the one in control.

Often, parents are quick to go into the child's room if they cry out at night. It is important to listen to your toddler's type of cry and become really tuned in to whether the little one is simply grizzling or, in fact, needs your help. Running in to a toddler's every whim can kick-start some pretty bad habits at sleeptime. Parents might find it hard to read their child well and they'll lose control of the bedtime situation. The little person becomes the one in charge!

Toddler twins and multiples

Often these toddlers – whether multiples or twins – may start the night off in separate beds, but are often found huddled together in one bed by morning time. It really is a 'twin thing' and, if I may say so, there's something really lovely about it.

And, as long as they are sleeping well, does it really matter whether your toddlers sleep together or in a bed on their own? Your babies will have simply gone from sharing a womb to sharing a bed; that's preferable to sharing their parents' bed, for reasons of physical space and the likely lack of sleep for everyone! If their night-time antics are causing problems, there are steps you can take, such as those in the case study below.

Case study: toddler trouble on the double

I received a lovely email from parents of twenty-one-month-old twins, Luke and Jenny. Their mum and dad had been struggling for some time with their sleep patterns. Neither of the twins had ever slept well at night and, as a result, neither had mum or dad. At the time, the children seemed, according to their mum, to be entering a new phase of sleep, so their parents felt it was a good time to start putting some sort of a plan in place. From a developmental point of view, the twins were both walking and communicating well. (I mention this because we have already talked about how developmental milestones can throw off a child's sleep patterns, and at this point we weren't expecting any huge changes in Luke and Jenny, from a developmental point of view.)

The email told their story. It is very detailed, which I love as it means I have lots of information to work on in order to put a plan together. I am giving you the long version, as it paints a good picture of all the things going on in their house to try to achieve the holy grail of sleep for everyone. The email read:

Both Luke and Jenny sleep in their own cots in separate rooms. Their rooms are side-by-side and they can often wake each other during the night.

The 'going to bed' routine is fairly consistent. They have their tea about 6. We move them into the playroom and gradually wind down the playing, change them for bed and turn on soft music. They finish with a story or stories by about 7.30.

It always takes both of us to get them down, as one goes with each child into their (separate) rooms.

They take a bottle on our lap until they fall asleep (this has been the routine since they were very small). Jenny usually nods off after a short time. Luke will often not go to sleep in the chair now, but on finishing his bottle or close to it he will point to his cot.

Once in the cot, he will look to hold onto his mum's hair. We have put down a pull-out bed for mum to lie on and Luke will put his arm out through the cot rails and reach (and pull) at his mum's hair. This worked for a while but now Luke will go through all of this and then stand up in the cot and look to come out and lie beside his mum on the foldout bed. Ordinarily, he will then fall asleep, holding mum's hair but sometimes will look for another bottle to do this. Luke is very disappointed by his dad's lack of hair during the night when he goes to resettle him!

Neither is sleeping past 1 a.m. before waking the whole house.

Jenny:

When we go in to settle her, she will cry and say 'chair, chair' to whoever is with her. If one of us sits in the chair Jenny will usually lie down, and occasionally will go back to sleep within a few minutes. However, it is becoming more usual for this to take up to an hour and sometimes this can even take 2 hours or more. On some nights, when we're particularly tired or have been up with Luke, we will just bring her into our bed.

Luke:

Luke will always look for a bottle to get back to sleep. Luke's night wakings can vary, usually from 12/1 a.m. onwards. He will look to get out of the cot and back onto the foldout bed with a bottle and some hair holding.

The Daytime:
Luke and Jenny attend crèche from 7.45 to 6.15, 2 days a week. The other 5 days they are at home.

So, as you can see, there was a lot going on here.

When we met, and as I listened to the twins' story, the main thing that stood out for me was the number of bottles being used to pacify the kids. These had become a big part of their bedtime and a huge sleep association for them. For a twenty-one-month-old I would normally expect a maximum of two bottles (if any at all) in a twenty-four-hour period. This pair of guzzlers could have been having five or more in a day!

We needed to stop this, and I remember their mum and dad being very anxious about it. I explained to them about using the art of distraction during the day, and encouraging the crèche not to be offering bottles to them either. These twins had a good and varied diet generally, and also drank plenty of water during the day, so I was not concerned that it was because they were hungry that they were drinking so much milk. It was simply their comfort and 'feel good' food. (As it turned out, the crèche staff explained that, in fact, Luke and Jenny were the only children of their age group having bottles, so the girls in the crèche were delighted to knock this on the head!)

I visited this family a few days after receiving their email and I met the two tiny messers, who were just lovely (if a little tired!). We discussed the bottle situation and a way of managing

Luke's love affair with his mum's hair. Hair pulling and stroking is not unusual in babies when they are falling asleep. So, we came up with a plan:

- I suggested that mum wear one of those nasty plastic swimming caps so that it becomes less attractive (and more difficult) for Luke to pull her hair.

- We decided to concentrate on the night-time antics with Luke and Jenny, and not to be overly concerned about daytime naps (particularly with Jenny).

- We also decided to move them both into beds and placed them together in one room. I felt that if we started training them in cots, Luke, in particular, might be inclined to get out of his, and we would have to move him to a bed anyway. Yes, they were young, but I was confident that not only the children, but also these parents, would be able to manage it. I was confident that the parents would follow through, whilst keeping the children safe.

The decision to move them into beds meant postponing the twins' training for a week or so while their parents sorted out the bedroom. In the meantime, I suggested that:

- They do their best to try and eliminate daytime bottles (and the middle-of-the-night one, if possible prior to starting training).

- They remove the 'bottle station' in their bedroom and limit all bottles to downstairs.

- They buy pillowcases and duvets that the twins could pick

themselves, giving them an opportunity to be involved in the new change.

- They invest in a large jar of coffee and remind themselves that they were simply taking back control of a situation that seemed (through months of sleep deprivation) to be out of hand. It just seemed harder (and it was) because there were two toddlers. In fact, if we had been able to take them individually, each would have been a textbook case!

A few weeks later I received a text from Luke and Jenny's mum letting me know that the beds were *in situ*. She and the twins' dad had been successful in eliminating the daytime bottles and were thrilled about it. They were ready to start on my technique, described previously.

The parents knew that this could potentially take a lot of effort, but once Luke and Jenny saw that their mum and dad were not changing their approach or, indeed, giving up, they would soon get the *consistent* message.

I also explained that, although generally the first night may be the hardest, occasionally children get such a surprise at the new approach and the novelty of a new bed, that they just go to sleep! But I wasn't counting on it with this pair.

Night one

Night one was *busy*! I am pretty sure Luke and Jenny's mum and dad got no sleep between them. But they phoned me the next day and were still upbeat and committed to working through this. The twins had not had any bottles during the night and, although mum and dad were in and out to them regularly, they remained in their room all night.

Night two

Night two was not quite as busy. The children fell asleep (Luke first, then Jenny) after around an hour or so at bedtime. Luke slept until 4 a.m. and even slept through an hour of Jenny giving out at around midnight!

Night three

Bedtime went very well. Both toddlers were asleep within forty minutes of going to bed. Luke woke at 1 a.m. His mum went to him twice (with two verbal responses), and he went back to sleep until almost 6 a.m. Jenny woke just after 2 a.m. She settled quickly enough, but woke again an hour later. She then slept until 7.15 a.m. Her mum and dad had to wake her, though, as they needed to get out to work.

Night four

Bedtime took only twenty minutes! The night was still a bit fractious, but there were no bottles and everyone slept in their own beds.

After a consistent and persistent week, Luke was sleeping through without waking or getting out of bed. Jenny would rouse at around 1 a.m. and go back to sleep pretty easily. She would then be in to her parents half an hour later for more of the same. But after this second visit, she would sleep till morning. Mum and dad were delighted with the change, and Jenny fell into line a few days later. They do say 'There's always one', don't they? It was simply a matter of ironing out the creases with Jenny.

Ultimately, we weren't aiming for perfection – what is that anyway? But what we achieved in terms of the goals we set out to reach was brilliant. We made dramatic progress, and all within a short time frame.

Separation anxiety and toddler sleep

Some children will start to exhibit signs of anxiety only at this stage (toddlerhood), whereas elements of anxiety can manifest themselves much earlier in other children.

Make a point of saying goodbye; do not sneak away, it's simply not fair. Toddlers know by now that you will be coming back to them. But they also know that a lot of noise will get a reaction, so they will probably throw in some drama for effect! That's not to say their feelings aren't real, though. Acknowledge this; remind your child that you will be back. Keep your promises.

What your toddler needs now is consistency. Do not change your normal routines or your approaches just because your child is going through a tough stage. Instead, focus on making the time you have together the best time ever. Make time spent together the time that counts most. Having extra one-on-one time with toddlers will help them build their confidence.

During the night, your little one may need extra comfort. Just be careful that you don't go on to create new bad habits in the process of comforting. So, for example, if your toddler starts waking at night, and you have never before brought the little one into your bed, then don't start doing so now! Comfort your toddler in his or her own room, and don't change what you used to do. You may have to spend a bit more time comforting your child, but that is okay. I don't mean that you should get up, read stories or watch TV to placate your toddler, but reassurance and your time might be just the ticket.

Toddlers and discipline: being firm, but fair

Quite often, part of the reason toddlers might put up a fight when it's time to go to bed is, simply put, because they can! Give an inch of freedom and those in the throes of the terrible twos will take a mile. And maybe a little bit more, for good measure! I feel it's important to state that when it comes to bedtime, the battle is worth having. Not least because these small 'terrorists' have probably ruled the roost for the most part during the day; to keep your sanity and retain some control, it is great to have at least one thing over which you as a parent have control.

All parents want the best for their children and they also want to enjoy them. Children go through so many wonderful phases and stages; it's only natural that parents would love it all to be a happy time. As children get older and develop a real sense of themselves, they may have other ideas! That's why it is so important that we as adults set boundaries and even have some discipline tools in place. Children can lose the run of themselves on occasion – often through no one's fault. It's up to us to rein them in occasionally.

When you choose a particular discipline tool it must be one that works for you and *your* family. There is no one-size-fits-all method of discipline for toddlers or young children. However, the more discipline tools you have at your disposal, the better. You may also need to adapt whatever technique you choose at a given time. Sometimes using one method alone will, over time, become ineffective. Keep a close eye on your child's reaction to your method of choice as time goes on. Is it becoming ineffective? Has the 'threat' or discipline method lost its lustre?

Most importantly, as with most things child-related, *be consistent* with your message. You want a particular behaviour to stop!

Selective ignoring

It is not always possible to ignore children when they are misbehaving, but sometimes the technique of selective ignoring works really well. If no one is in danger of being hurt, then not drawing any attention to what's going on can be highly effective. (This is similar to the technique I advise at bedtime, whereby you don't entertain any messing as such and only address the situation if your child is upset.) Toddlers will soon learn that they are not going to get a reaction to their bad or negative behaviour and will, more often than not, stop what they are doing just as quickly as they started.

It is certainly not my intention to come across as 'mean' in suggesting that you ignore your child, so please don't get me wrong! You are being asked to ignore the *behaviour* – which is probably being shown to you only to get some form of attention. To a child, all attention (both positive and negative) is attention nonetheless. Try not to get emotionally involved with the behaviour your child is displaying. Your toddler might say that 'mummy/daddy is stupid', or 'I don't love you any more', for example, but don't take it personally!

Distraction

If you start to see your toddler about to misbehave and notice that 'mischievous glint in their eye', intercept the little one! Find something to distract your child. For example: One of your children is happily playing with a puzzle. You spot your toddler eyeing this child up, and you just know he's on the way over to bother his sibling. Step in and distract your toddler before they make contact. Offer them their own puzzle and breathe a sigh of relief that you may perhaps have just averted the Third World War!

I am all in favour of letting little ones work out the power of sharing for themselves, but for the times when you don't have the time or energy to deal with potential meltdowns, distraction just might be the answer!

Dealing with temper tantrums

Dealing with temper tantrums can often be a challenging area. I propose a few ways of trying to manage them.

Initially, you could try selective ignoring, as mentioned earlier. These tantrum meltdowns might end rapidly once your toddler sees that you are no longer paying attention or trying to negotiate with him or her. If your toddler is in a safe place I recommend that you just let the little one go for it. This allows toddlers to express their emotions and, however difficult it may seem, try not to get involved. Stop worrying about everyone else's opinion; chances are you may never see the bystanders again anyway!

If the tantrum persists, offer your child a few words of support and encouragement, whilst making sure that you are not adding fuel to the fire. Sometimes engaging with your little one in the middle of a tantrum will simply make things worse, as they can often sense your own unease in the situation. If they see that you are not really entertained by the 'show', they will likely just get over it and forget about it as quickly as it started! Toddlers understand verbal directions (and the tone in which they are given) a lot more than they are given credit for, and, for the most part, they are well aware of what they are doing.

A typical example where toddlers would famously throw a tantrum would be in a supermarket. I suggest you try to pre-empt and avoid this happening by giving them jobs to do while you are there. Make them responsible for collecting certain items for you on your way around the shop. It will give them a role to play and once occupied with 'a job' they are less likely to get fed up/bored during the shopping trip.

Avoiding being caught up in the small stuff

Learn how to distinguish between behaviours that are serious and dangerous and those that are less likely to become big issues. By getting caught up in the small stuff, you may send out a confused message to your toddler. Your child will not understand the things that are important to you and the expectations you have about things that really matter. Ignore behaviours that are of low-level importance to you and save your energy for the more important issues.

In short, ignore petty sibling arguments and react to the times when your children are being physical or hurting each other. The latter behaviour is obviously more dangerous than the former.

Case study
My dad: 'That's right. Go on. Have a good go!'

My mum recently reminded me of a time when my two sisters were around seven and four years of age. Mum said she was coming down the stairs with her hands full (probably carrying the laundry basket) and she stumbled upon the two girls having a pretty intense argument over a hairbrush. They had been fighting with each other all day so it was not an unusual scene!

Just as mum was about to involve herself in the fracas, my father came out of the kitchen with a cup of coffee in his hand and *The Irish Times* under his arm. He passed by the pair of them on his way to the sitting room and, without looking at either of them, said, 'That's right. Go on. Have a good go!' For a moment mum thought she had better intervene, but instead decided to pass by them. When she came back out a few minutes later the two of them were laughing and had totally forgotten the row!

The point is, I think, that very often parents will intervene when it's not helpful. Sometimes there is more learning for the kids when they can work it out for themselves. As long as there is no bullying involved, and these little scraps are isolated incidents, there is a lot to be learned from sometimes leaving children to their own devices.

Setting limits

For older toddlers and young children, offer ultimatums. For example, 'If you do not eat your dinner, then you may not watch TV later.' Be specific and don't make empty threats. Follow through on your words. Children have a great knack of remembering all the times when you don't stick to your guns!

Time out/space to think

Time out or thinking space can also be very useful if you are trying to diffuse a situation. It allows the toddler (and you) to step away from what was causing the behaviour in the first place. It gives toddlers an opportunity to think about why they are being 'punished' or removed and, over time, will lessen the likelihood of a repeat performance.

Take, for example, a time when your child might be hitting you or another child. Sometimes, even after you tell your child to stop a number of times, the little one may continue to hit whilst looking you in the eye and even grinning! This can be really infuriating. Give your child a warning: 'If you hit again, you will go on time out/go to the thinking space.' Should your toddler continue, then it is up to you to follow through. Give the little one the time out (one minute per year of age), ask for an apology, and get on with your day. Don't hold grudges; they are pointless and just use up your precious energy!

It's important to note here that the bedtime battle is *not* the time for using one of the discipline tools outlined above. I recall a story of one little person who was putting up fairly strong resistance to staying in her bed in the middle of the night. Her determined dad was dealing with the situation as best he could, but despite his insistence that she go back to sleep, this little girl was having none of it. Out of sheer desperation, he took her downstairs and used their time out place on the bottom step of the stairs. As he sat there with her, he realised, 'This is ridiculous. She thinks we are up for the day now and is wide awake. Worse still, I am wide awake too!' So, it was back to bringing her to bed in silence. Eventually his persistence paid off and the house went back to some semblance of calm. He was more annoyed with himself for deviating from their plan than he was with her for pushing him so far!

And yes, toddlers will push and push and push!

Case study: the big boy bed hopper

Bedtime issues are not limited to babies and toddlers. One of my first experiences of an older child with sleep issues was Marcus. Mind you, he didn't feel like he had any sleep issues at all. He was having a wonderful time hopping in and out of his parents' bed at the ripe old age of four!

In any case, his dad got in touch. He felt unsure of whether he was confessing the world's worst sin to me or actually doing the right thing! As always, I reminded him that what works for you as a family is *always* the right thing. The problem was, this wasn't working any more. And after almost four years of very little sleep, this really wasn't ideal!

When Marcus was born, he slept in a Moses basket beside his parents, but once he got too big for that he moved into their bed. Not the end of the world, but this may have kick-started the eventual issues. During that first year, they tried almost everything to get Marcus to sleep in his cot, even resorting one night to climbing into it beside him. But more often than not, Marcus and his mum ended up sharing a bed while his dad was evicted to the spare room!

Coupled with the desire to sleep next to his mum, Marcus also had a thing for eyebrows! He loved to rub other people's eyebrows as a comfort thing. It didn't seem to matter who they belonged to, either! So having a good bushy set of eyebrows close by at bedtime meant that some sleep was achieved.

Although his mum and dad accepted that they were mostly responsible for Marcus' night-time antics, they were also aware that Marcus had a huge part to play. He would do anything and everything to get them to stay in his room while he slept, even one night going so far as to explain that Paddington Bear needed the bathroom ... urgently! In fairness to Marcus, there really were no set limits as to what was expected of him at bedtime, so it wasn't fair to chastise.

Having gone through the story and giving it a little perspective, we formulated a plan for Marcus and his parents. This was definitely not a discipline issue. He would not be punished for doing wrong, but we would be gently guiding him towards a new behaviour and teaching him how to settle on his own – on a gentle learning curve that wouldn't leave him scarred for life.

I advised the parents to use the same method for putting Marcus to bed and for resettling him during the night. I likened it to teaching him to walk or ride a bike – slowly releasing their grasp, with a little less support, each time they went to comfort him. They liked my suggested method as, in their words, they felt it 'wasn't as mad as controlled crying insofar as we were not counting minutes of him crying before we could go into him, which always seems a bit cold and calculated'.

They were to have the same bedtime routine as they always did. They would kiss him goodnight after his story and walk out. If he followed them, they were to bring him back to his own bed for as many times as it took, only speaking to reassure him during the first two times. After that – radio silence! If he was crying in his bed before going to sleep, or if he woke and started crying during the night, they were to use their heads and listen to 'how' he was crying. If they felt that he was getting upset, they were to go in, but the majority of the time his cries were just last-ditch, half-hearted attempts to get them back into the room; when they ignored those he got bored and went back to sleep every time.

Marcus' father relayed the details of the training back to me in a series of texts and emails. Here is how it went.

Night one – Friday
Upstairs at 7.15 p.m. Did routine (i.e. teeth, toilet, pyjamas, milk and a story, main light out, kiss and walk out of room). He followed us out and we brought him back 6 or 7 times. Cried a bit last 3 times, and then settled himself. Snoring by 8.10 p.m. He woke at 2 a.m. and I had to bring him back 5 or 6 times with him staying there for 5 or 10 minutes at a time. He was up once or twice more during the night but nothing major. The next morning he came in to us at 7.30 a.m.

Night two – Saturday
Upstairs at 7.15 p.m. and start routine. In bed by 7.30 and asleep 7.45. Only came out once, still trying 'phantom poo'. Then woke at 8.20 p.m. crying. Seemed distressed. Went in. He was sitting up in bed sweating as he was just too hot. Quickly went back to sleep, small whimper. Turned heating off. He didn't wake until 4.45 and I spent an hour going back

and forth but once he settled he slept again until 8 a.m. Great success by all accounts.

Night three – Sunday

Upstairs at 7.30 p.m. In bed by 7.45 p.m. and he went straight to sleep and never came out. He woke then about 12 and whimpered a bit being brought back and forth until 1 a.m. but then slept right through until 7.30 a.m. Definitely getting there and we are delighted.

Night four – Monday

Upstairs by 7.45 p.m. In bed by 8 p.m. and again went straight to sleep. He has just woken up crying now as I type this but mum has it under control as we were expecting he might try a night like this – last attempt to win back the night. We are all over this – with no small amount of thanks to Niamh.

Marcus' parents genuinely haven't looked back. Their little guy has started school now and is a well-rested, happy child (with well-rested, happy parents!).

Toddlers have their very own opinions … about everything! You can enjoy that about them – just not at bedtime. Bedtimes need not be battle times.

We have now covered the techniques for young and older babies in cots and those toddlers jumping in and out of bed. Still, in terms of childhood sleep there can be hurdles we don't expect. These unexpected night-time dramas can prove to be challenging and can throw your night-times into further disarray.

7

SLEEP DISORDERS AND THINGS THAT GO BUMP IN THE NIGHT

Are you upset little friend? Have you been lying awake worrying? Well, don't worry ... I'm here. The flood waters will recede, the famine will end, the sun will shine tomorrow, and I will always be here to take care of you.

Charles M. Schulz

Sleep disturbances and disorders

Sleep coaching or training will not be the answer to every sleep problem, so it is important to be aware of some other sleep issues that are not caused by 'poor habits' but are in fact real, and quite often medical, sleep disorders. This section will touch once more on the 'science bit'.

I believe that having an awareness of these sleep issues is important. Lots of children experience a sleep disorder at some stage in their childhood, and most of us will have heard of (or indeed experienced) some of the more familiar ones, including night terrors.

First things first, though. If you feel that your child is experiencing a sleep issue that is bigger than simply not having established good habits over time, then my advice would be to talk to your doctor or paediatrician about this. Once you have a diagnosis, there will be help out there for you.

Sleep disturbance and sleep disorder: the differences

A sleep disturbance is usually a disruption to the manner in which someone falls asleep in the first instance, and their ability to either stay asleep or get back to sleep at a later stage. Children with sleep disturbance issues are unlikely to require medical intervention.

A sleep disorder is more likely to have a more clinical or medical explanation. Many people with sleep disorders may not even know that they have them and may be diagnosed only after complaints of feeling continually exhausted after a seemingly full night's sleep. Children, and indeed adults, who show signs of the more serious sleep disorders, will normally have undergone some form of medical intervention. In saying this, not all disorders require professional help and parents can effectively help their child cope with those that do not.

Arousal disorders

Nightmares

Nightmares are, in fact, technically not a sleep disorder, but a sleep disturbance. But they can be very disruptive, and also frightening or upsetting for children and parents. They tend to occur in the later part of the night (after midnight). They are not always restricted to this phase of sleep, but are just more likely to happen then.

Typically, your child will have a bad dream and wake up frightened or upset. The little one may call for you and be crying, but will be able to explain what happened and will be relatively easy to console and comfort.

Children process the activities of the day while they are asleep and are affected in different ways by what they have seen or heard. Something that seems innocuous at the time – such as a TV pro-gramme – can lead to unprocessed fears, which surface in the child while they sleep. It is important to know that many children will go into a deep phase of sleep in the early hours of the morning (4 a.m. or 5 a.m.) and may have a small arousal from their sleep just before that. These nightmares may also occur at this time, so it's important not to confuse this with your child's simply wanting to get up and start the day!

Management of nightmares

Try to avoid scary or overstimulating experiences during the day.

Reduce any stressors – those things that cause anxiety in your child. Remember that all children are different, so just because one child is not afraid of *Dora the Explorer*, doesn't mean that another child won't have fears resulting from watching a particu-lar episode!

Ensure your little ones are getting adequate sleep (both at night and throughout the day) – that is enough sleep for their age and stage (see figure 5 on p. 46). An overtired child is more likely to experience more of the active sleep phases (REM sleep) and therefore may be more at risk of having nightmares.

Treatment of nightmares

Try to strike a balance between reassurance and excessive atten-tion. Calm your child in his or her own bed or cot, and resist the urge to bring the little one to your bed if it is not what you would normally do. When your child wakes, go and comfort him or her. Explain that it wasn't real and that it was just a dream. Do your best to try to reassure your child that everything is okay.

Whilst this is not the case with night terrors, children will remember that the bad dream happened. They may not remember exact details about it, but they will be aware that they were disrupted. If your child does recall the reason for the dream, use creative play the following day to talk through the nightmare with the little one. Activities like drawing and story time about dreams can be really useful.

Be imaginative. Earlier, when I discussed toddler bedtime antics, I mentioned (in 'Tips for toddler sleep') using a squirty bottle to make a magic spray that children can use to get rid of the 'bad scary' things from their rooms at bedtime. The contents of the bottle are unimportant. I suggest you have nothing in it at all – it is so utterly magic that it is, in fact, invisible spray. Call it 'monster spray' or 'animal spray' – whatever it is that is frightening your child. It gives these little ones a sense of control over things that feel outside their comfort zones. A little responsibility can go a long way.

Note: It is not unusual for younger children, even babies, to experience nightmares, although with these younger babies you will naturally be less likely to be able to manage nightmares as easily as you can with older children who can communicate with you. It is more likely that the cause of these nightmares in younger children will be less to do with factors such as screen time and more likely to be a little more 'internal'. Things like separation anxiety can play a part here, or sudden changes in their lives –

starting crèche, for example, or moving house. For younger babies, ensuring a quiet and calm bedtime can really help, as can a routine that remains the same or, at least, very similar, each night.

Night terrors

Night terrors are far more distressing to watch than nightmares, particularly for a parent. They are a recognised sleep disorder, unlike nightmares.

Night terrors tend to happen at the start of the night, so in general they will occur before you have gone to bed yourself. Although it may seem like your child has woken up from sleep, the little one is actually only partially awake and yet can be thrashing around the bed/cot. Providing comfort and trying to 'snap the child out of it' will probably make no real difference to your child at the time. Children are normally quite unaware of the experience and generally they will have no memory of their night terrors having occurred at all.

Management of night terrors

The best way to manage a night terror is primarily by making the child's sleep space a safe place. Children with night terrors will be extremely physically active and can be jumping around their beds quite frantically. Extra cushions and pillows on the floor and around the bed can help reduce injury. Make sure they are comfortable, but don't try and wake them – it will be even more distressing for them. Be there, but allow them to 'come out of it' themselves.

If your child is experiencing a phase of these night terrors, there is generally no point in discussing it with the little one the following day. Bear in mind that your child won't remember, and if you start talking to them about the fact that he or she was scream-ing and shouting and bouncing around the room, you may actu-ally scare your child further.

Treatment of night terrors

One solution which parents find works really well is to wake your child shortly before the 'expected terror'. It is likely that your child experiences a terror at roughly the same time every night (it is usually pre-midnight for most). So, if your child has been hav-ing terrors at around 10 p.m. each night for a number of nights, I would suggest that you rouse the little one around 9.30 p.m. and have a short little chat or offer a drink of water. You are rou-sing them enough to break the sleep cycle, so the pattern is dis-rupted in the hope that your child will simply 'skip' the terror and continue on with the sleep. It is also a good idea to waken the child again later in the night. Regular or scheduled 'wakings' can be really effective in dealing with terrors in the short term. But, should they continue, I would seek a medical opinion.

Comparison of nightmares and night terrors
Nightmares

- Occur in REM sleep (active sleep).
- Occur during late sleep phase (late at night/early morning).
- Distressing for parents and children.
- Less motor activity – child probably not thrashing around but upset and possibly frightened.
- Less likely to result in injury.

- Child has memory of the event, but might not remember exactly what it is that has woken him or her.

Night terrors

- Occur in non-REM sleep (deep sleep).

- Occur during early sleep phase (early part of the night).

- Very distressing for parents; less so for the children.

- Child very active.

- Incidents may cause injury as child may be thrashing around uncontrollably.

- For the most part, child will not remember events (although parents will probably never forget it).

Sleepwalking

Again, this is something that many parents will have experienced with their little people. It is more common with school-age children than with toddlers and pre-schoolers. Episodes of sleepwalking tend to disappear or resolve themselves once the teenage years hit. However, sleepwalking may rear its head again in adulthood, particularly during any times of stress.

Repeated or scheduled waking can help disrupt sleepwalking (as in the event of night terrors), but just make sure that your child is safe. Place stair gates on your stairs, and perhaps lock the doors to rooms where your child might be in danger.

I have heard of older children – these would be extreme cases – who might go to the kitchen and prepare food for themselves at night during a sleepwalking episode. Kitchen knives are a dangerous toy for a sleeping, but moving, child. Lock everything away. It is better to be safe than sorry.

Bedwetting

This also falls into the category of sleep disorders and is more likely to occur during that non-REM part of sleep, pre-midnight.

Reducing fluid intake in the afternoon and evenings, and indeed 'lifting' little ones to go to the toilet before you go to bed, can help put a stop to this – although it may only be a short-term solution. My advice, if bedwetting persists into early childhood (past five or six years of age), would be to consult with your GP or paediatrician.

In general, children 'grow out' of this phase, but it is important to realise that – like any other disorder listed – it is out of their control. They are not doing this on purpose or for attention. Do not chastise them for it. They simply can't help it.

Sleep-onset disorders

These disorders are different from arousal disorders in that they are almost always limited to the manner in which a child falls asleep. They can happen when little ones experience a lot of difficulty in getting off to sleep in the first place.

Although many sleep-onset disorders are quite harmless, they can be quite disturbing for parents. However, for some reason it is one of the only ways their little one can fall asleep. These disorders can include, for example, quite energetically rocking on all fours in order to fall asleep, banging their heads on cot railings, chanting quite loudly, and making all sorts of noises. Sometimes, this becomes a child's normal pattern, rather than being a difficulty for the little one. As long as children are safe, I am not too concerned about these as children tend to grow out of them. They are usually trying to process the events of the day. As children get older, and if the disorder seems to become a bigger problem, some behavioural therapies to help them with their coping skills can be really effective.

Sleep apnoea

Sleep apnoea is often thought of by parents as simply repeated waking and, therefore, wrongly treated with some sleep-training techniques. But sleep apnoea needs to be diagnosed by a GP or paediatrician. It is more often found in overweight men, but sleep apnoea can happen with young children too. An apnoea occurs where the brain forgets to tell the body to breathe for a short period. Then, the child will start breathing again with quite a startle.

Sleep apnoea is caused by breathing difficulties due to a possible obstruction. Children with these difficulties may snore quite loudly, or may breathe with their mouths open whilst they sleep. They may also be extremely tired during the day, because they are often jolted out of their sleep at night; they don't really experience good-quality sleep, resulting in their feeling exhausted during the day. So, even though they may not be bothering parents at night, they are not having good restful sleep.

Sleep apnoea can be eased by having your tonsils out or adenoids removed. In worse-case scenarios, there is a breathing machine called a CPAP, which involves wearing a breathing mask at night in order to assist with keeping breathing patterns more regular.

I know that this all sounds very dangerous, but it really should be something of which parents are aware. People's lives are not at immediate risk directly from having a sleep apnoea, but the knock-on effect of stopping breathing regularly during the night can seriously impact health. That is why, if you suspect your child may have this problem, you should go to see your GP or paediatrician.

Narcolepsy

Narcolepsy is a very rare condition in which people have an uncontrollable urge to sleep. It is potentially very dangerous, as they can fall asleep at any time and place. Narcolepsy requires medical intervention.

If you are making your way through this book, it is highly unlikely that narcolepsy would be a problem for you! I am including it here simply as part of general information on the topic of sleep disorders. Should I come across it in my practice, I would always recommend a consultation with a paediatrician or medical specialist.

So, whilst the last few disorders are relatively uncommon, they are really worth mentioning. Like I have said, they are all manageable and/or treatable either through medical intervention or some simple adjustments to sleep habits.

8

TIME CHANGES, TRAVELLING AND HOSPITAL STAYS

He who would travel happily must travel light.

Antoine de Saint-Exupéry

Time changes: spring forward/fall back

The best way to approach the seasonal time change (when the clocks go back or forward) is without fear. Face it head on. Whether you like it or not, this adjustment is going to happen, but it is not out of our control entirely. As adults, we become obsessed with the number of hours sleep we get. Infants are reliant on our guidance and we can help them manage this.

So, a few days before the clocks go forward in spring, start putting your little one to bed fifteen minutes earlier each day. But do get your child up at the same time each morning. That way, by the time the clocks actually change, the child has adjusted without much of a fuss.

A few days before the autumn change, start putting your child down to bed fifteen minutes later each night. Perhaps start on the Wednesday before the clocks go back. So, by the Saturday night your little one will be going an hour later than at the start of the week. There's no point putting children down too much later than their normal bedtime – quite often they will be overtired and the wheels will fall off! Again, get them up at the same time each morning. That way, by the time the clocks actually change, the child has no idea.

It is not too late after the event – so even if you forget until clock-changing D-Day, you should catch up within a week.

Travel and holidays with toddlers and young babies

Once holiday time approaches, we all begin to look forward to getting a break away from our normal lives. We have our own ideas about what the perfect holiday might be, but chances are we may have to adapt this (and often quite a lot) if we have small children to think about.

Remember that babies and toddlers love routine and are not big fans of change. It is not fair to expect them to be happy with your choice of holiday destination if their 'normal day to day' does not fit in with the overall plan.

Invest in a baby carrier

Baby carriers and slings are an ideal way to travel with babies and toddlers. Investing in a good-quality carrier can solve lots of problems when you travel. I think they are ideal for weekend city breaks where you don't want to be bringing the cumbersome pram around with you everywhere. Many cities are full of steps and winding streets that are definitely more awkward to navigate with a buggy. Babies will sleep happily in their carriers, and toddlers too. You can find comfortable slings for younger babies, and there are also some fabulous carriers for toddlers that you can wear like a backpack. Your toddler will be up high on your back and have a great view!

If you are going away for a longer time, buy a cheap, light-weight buggy that reclines easily. You may be out in the evenings for meals and the little one can happily sleep in the buggy while you eat and can be transferred into a cot when you get home.

What to bring

Find out about your sleeping arrangements before you go. Most holiday destinations will provide travel cots if you ask for them. I would suggest you bring your own mattress (they can fold up quite nicely) as mattress safety is very important. You might want to bring your own bedclothes – maybe a familiar duvet cover for your child.

If your little one still takes a daytime nap, and usually does this in a dark room, you can bring strips of blackout material with you to use. Alternatively, ask the hotel to put black sacks on the windows! Also, bring a blackout cover for your buggy if you are expecting your little one to sleep in it during the day or if you are out for a meal at night. It can be a godsend.

Bring your child's gro-bag if you use one, as it will be a familiar part of the bedtime routine.

Sleeping arrangements

If your child doesn't normally sleep in your room, but you will be sharing on holidays, it would be an idea to position the cot as far as possible from your bed. This will cause the least disruption.

If your child is waking at night while away and you wouldn't normally bring him or her into your bed, try not to do so on holidays. By the time you go home your little one will think this is the new way of sleeping and you might have a battle on your hands!

Taking flight

Try to get the timing of your flights as appropriate for your child's routine as possible. Don't delay nap times in the hope that your child might sleep on the flight. It is better to have a child who is alert and happy than one who is overtired and miserable. It can be distressing for everyone, and not exactly an ideal start to your family holiday.

Flying can be hard enough when you are an adult, but if you're two years old and have to cross international time zones, it can be a bit trickier!

The advantage of being able to board first with small children can be diminished by their getting 'cabin fever' before they've even taken off; also, planes can be very hot, which makes everyone cranky. A few options are available: board the plane as late as possible, which helps limit the cabin fever; send one parent ahead to get set up (this is particularly relevant when there are lots of bags to be stored overhead, but is possible only if two adults are travelling); or go to the plane together, with one parent standing with the kids at the door of the plane (on the gangway) where it is cooler and there's the distraction of the other passengers boarding.

Keep your children entertained

Children's attention spans are notoriously short – an eighteen-month-old has an average attention span of two to three minutes and a three- to four-year-old can usually pay attention for about ten minutes. Sounds scary when you have an eight-hour flight ahead of you! Pack sticker books, colouring books and finger puppets or small dolls your children can cuddle and look after on the journey. If you are lucky enough to have a portable DVD player, bring it with you! You won't be frowned upon for being a bad parent. Neighbouring passengers may in fact thank you! Use whatever resources you can to get your children through the flight.

Make sure you differentiate between your expectations and your children's expectations. It is likely that your children will be quite content with you and their toys, as long as you are stress-free and happy. If the wheels are falling off, introduce a new toy at the 'lowest point' of the flight, that is, when you can't distract them any further.

Keep hydrated

We all know that air travel tends to dehydrate us and dry out our skin. Kids aren't immune to this, so remember to keep them hydrated too. Make sure your children are drinking as much as you are and give them plenty of water before they sleep.

Although you may be restricted from bringing bottled water on the flight, if you are travelling long haul most airlines are pretty good about providing water. Take it when it is offered.

Eat lightly

One of the ways our bodies tell the time is through food and eating habits, so when you travel to a different time zone with your kids, it is often recommended that you eat your meals at the correct local time in order to adjust more easily to jet lag. If, for example, your children's dinner arrives on the plane and it is actually breakfast time at your destination, encourage your children to eat lightly and to eat as much fruit and vegetables as possible.

Airline food is not known for being light and delicious, so bring plenty of fruit snacks in your carry-on luggage. Grapes are ideal, as they rehydrate the body. Good alternatives are pieces of melon, pineapple, raisins and dried mango.

Jet lag and sleep

Jet lag is always worse going east, so travelling west generally requires less of an adjustment than travelling east. Thankfully, if you come home to Ireland from west to east, you will be returning to a place that is familiar to your kids, so hopefully the normality of life at home will help to smooth the process and get sleep routines firmly back on track!

Whether going away or coming back though, don't think about where you've come from – think about where you are going and anticipate the changing time zones. For journeys to Europe there will be only little adjustments required, as in general the time difference is not more than two hours either way. So, forget about where you were yesterday and try to keep naptimes at local time. The same applies to bedtime – you may rise early the first couple of mornings, but things should settle down after a day or so and you will all have adjusted your body clocks.

When you arrive, get plenty of fresh air for yourself and, especially, the little ones. Go and explore and keep the little ones active and occupied.

If your flight arrives at night-time (locally), use minimal lights and keep the house dark! Trick the children's minds a little bit.

Stick to your routine, regardless of time. If, on the first night, the kids wake at 4 a.m., get up and have breakfast and continue the day as normal. You can slowly adjust their sleeps and meal-times as the days go by.

It will take at least three days to settle, so don't expect too much too soon from your children.

If you have travelled long haul, try to stay awake as long as possible. Forget the time zone you have left behind and focus on where you are now. When you get home, don't expect your little ones to adjust to time zones immediately. In general, for every hour of time difference, it will take roughly that amount of days to recover. For example, if there was a five-hour time difference between home and your holiday spot, then it will generally take five days to adjust!

A hospital stay and the impact on sleep

Children's sleep habits may be disrupted by a serious illness, or indeed an unexpected or extended hospital stay. These can have a detrimental effect on both sleep and family life.

Many babies and toddlers will regress to almost 'new baby' sleep after a serious illness. Once they are healthy again, and are ready to come home, their previously good sleep habits might go out the window. They (and you) will find this change a particular challenge.

Hospitals are notoriously busy places. The bright lights and various machines beeping all through the day and night can cause your infant or toddler's body clock to need a little tweaking once you bring the little one home. The coming and going of nurses and doctors during this time can be very disruptive, as can different tests and procedures.

In hospital many babies, toddlers and young children will need medication (antibiotics and pain medication to help their little bodies fight off whatever is wrong with them). They may even need sedation to get them through whatever has caused them to be admitted to hospital. If your child has been sedated, 'waking up' in an unfamiliar environment is very frightening. If the little one has wires and tubes to deal with, even more so.

While your child is in the hospital, you can do a few things to help keep some sense of normality:

- Never leave without letting your baby or toddler know that you will be back. So, don't leave while your child is sleeping. It is simply unfair and can be frightening.

- Bring in some familiar things from home – teddies, blankets, books, etc. – to give your child a sense of security and familiarity.

- Limit the number of visitors – too many people at one time is daunting. The same applies to staff. It is okay to ask them to try not to have too many nurses or doctors come in to your child's space at any given time. All these new faces take a lot of getting used to, and limiting numbers will allow your little one to form a few one-to-one relationships with them, particularly if your child will be in hospital for a while. Hospital protocols have to be taken into account, but it is okay to raise any concerns about your own child.

Once children are well enough to come home, many parents find that even though they try to keep the bedtime routine the same as it was before, things have changed and new needs will surface:

- Your child may need you to stay with him or her when falling asleep – which makes sense if you were by your child's bedside while the little one was in hospital.

- Your child may seem more anxious at bedtime. Again this makes sense. In hospital the unfamiliar noises and different faces (doctors, nurses and hospital staff) around them can often be unnerving and your child will certainly have memories of the experience. This is especially the case if your little one required many tests, and every time he or she turned around someone else was producing a needle for blood work or to give medication!

- Your child may start to manifest different behaviour during the day and may start to refuse naps.

- Your child may start to wake hourly and not be able to adjust to the changing sleep cycles. Over time, and once the little one starts to feel secure again at home, this will start to progress and will eventually go back to being close to perfect, with your support and encouragement.

Case study: one parent's tale of a hospital stay

A close friend of mine experienced the disturbance, and indeed trauma, wrought by an emergency visit to hospital a couple of years ago. Her daughter Nikki, a healthy eighteen-month-old, was admitted to hospital with pneumonia. Unfortunately, things deteriorated rather rapidly and this little girl was sedated in order to allow her body to fight the infection. She was, essentially, in an induced coma. It was a very traumatic time for everyone, particularly for her devoted parents. Just short of a week later, the doctors were happy to take her off sedation. And, thankfully, within days, her recovery was going so well that she was allowed home.

Her mum recalled the nightmare sleep scenarios that ensued. She felt it was similar to having a newborn all over again, as Nikki's sleep habits were all over the place. Although torn between being elated that her little girl was well again, and also being exhausted from the trauma surrounding everything that had happened in such a short space of time, she asked me about training her to sleep again. I was quite hesitant to offer any coaching advice. This little girl, and her family, had gone through enough. The only thing they all needed now was extra TLC and lots of comfort.

My friend wrote to me explaining some of the things she wished she had known. It is so honest and raw that it is worth sharing:

I wish I knew that any child who has spent time in intensive care and indeed in a coma will come home like a newborn, and that they need full sleep training all over again. They have lost synch with their body clock. Daytime becomes night-time and night-time becomes daytime.

I wish I knew that, most of all, our daughter was going to have severe anxiety stemming from the side effects of drug withdrawal. Had I known this beforehand I would have reset my expectations, and resisted becoming frustrated by the incessant waking up and calling out for 'mummy' through the night.

I wish I had listened to those people, when she was in a coma, who said, 'You can do nothing to change the situation, so while she "sleeps" you should sleep too.' I didn't. I stayed awake day and night watching every tube, monitor and apparatus beep.

When she did finally 'wake', I was emotionally and physically exhausted, with little or no strength to carry me through her recovery, when she actually needed me the most.

I wish I knew about the incredible strain, on coming home, that now I had a child that couldn't sleep and all I wanted to do was sleep. Not a good combination for a traumatised and recovering family. I wish I had known what a strain the sleep deprivation would bring on our entire family.

I did not anticipate that an illness could not only bring a family so close together but also push everyone apart. Thoughts of blame, how it could have been avoided and all the 'what if' scenarios are a destructive recipe for any couple or family.

Learning to address what happens when a child is very sick and acknowledging everyone's feelings is so important.

How ironic it is now that I wish I could go back to that time in ICU, when I promised I would never take anything in life for granted again, never scold my children for acting out, never be so dismissive when all they want me to do is look and listen. How ironic that life simply goes on and suddenly you find yourself back in that place of 'busy-ness' and activity, hurrying around with life's chores and forgetting to just stop, take stock of everything you have and be grateful.

We were told that we would go through five phases: denial, acceptance, depression, understanding and then happiness again. This couldn't be truer. You just don't realise or accept it at the time.

Over time, Nikki was able to get back on track, thanks in no small part to the support and comfort she was given by her parents.

In short, following a hospital stay, give yourself time to get through the various stages, with patience, deep breaths and a lot of love.

And I am very happy to report that Nikki is now resettled into her lovely sleep patterns and everyone is reaping the benefits again of a decent night's sleep!

A long-term hospital stay (or indeed a shorter one) is many parents' worst nightmare and while often there is little you can do while your child remains in the care of the doctors and nurses, once you are home and have put the emotional demons to bed, normal life can resume.

FINAL MESSAGE

A baby is born with a need to be loved, and never outgrows it.

Frank A. Clark

I hope you can now see the light at the end of the tunnel and that this book has given you the confidence to move forward and start to make some positive changes.

Techniques and routines can be really helpful in establishing good sleep habits for your little people. It doesn't really matter when you start to implement them, though, so pick an age or stage and then adjust accordingly. You won't regret it.

Like most new things, they won't fall into place immediately. Allow some time for changes to take hold. More often than not, a slow and gentle start will yield better long-term success.

But I want you to know this much:

You never screw up.

You just love them.

That's what counts.

APPENDIX 1

SAMPLE SLEEP DIARIES

If your child is experiencing sleep problems, try filling in the sleep diaries here for a week. It might help you identify any changes needed to your child's routine. It can also be useful to have a record of how many times your baby woke up at night and how you managed to settle the little one back to sleep.

Not only will it let you see if there is a pattern emerging, but you will also be able to record feeding (solids and liquids) and also nappy changes.

Day One: Daytime routine			
Activity	*Time*	*Related Information*	
Woke up for the day			
Feed/bottle		How much taken?	
Morning nap		Where?	
		How long for?	
Feed/bottle		How much taken?	

Lunch			
Lunchtime nap		Where?	
		How long for?	
Feed/bottle		How much taken?	
Afternoon nap		Where?	
		How long for?	
Tea			
Feed/bottle		How much taken?	
Bed		How did you settle baby?	

Any other notes (e.g. bowel movements, anything that happened during the day that was 'out of the ordinary')

Night One: Bedtime and Waking		
Bedtime @ _____ p.m.		
Time baby woke up	How long awake?	How you settled baby

Appendix 2

TESTIMONIALS

We used to dread going to bed.

After spending two years being woken up several times every night by our youngest daughter, we could no longer function properly. Help arrived in the shape of Niamh. From the moment we met, we were reassured that our lives would change for the better. How true this turned out to be. Niamh reviewed our daughter's bedtime routine and made some common sense changes to provide us with a proper structure. The results were startling. With some work, patience and persistence, by night three our daughter slept through the night for the first time in two years (and so did we). Niamh provided constant support throughout the whole process and kept us focused through the tougher moments. Don't get me wrong, our daughter has her moments, but this no longer fazes us! We know what we are doing and we are confident in the process.

To anyone who is experiencing sleeping difficulties with their children I would say stop what you are doing and enlist the help of Niamh. Like us, you will never look back.

C., Dublin

I would like to share my story about how Niamh has helped me and her complete love of her work helping families. I first contacted Niamh when my son was four weeks old. I was at my wits' end from lack of sleep and my three-year-old daughter feeling like she was totally put out from the arrival of her new baby brother.

My daughter was a total textbook baby and I thought my son would fall into a routine as easily as she did but I couldn't have been more wrong. My son had a great daytime routine and cluster fed all night long and as I was breastfeeding I was so worn out. I started to offer bottles to see would it help. I tried every trick in the book and nothing worked. I emailed Niamh and she phoned me back the next morning. I was over the moon to say the least when I heard her voice and her kind words that I was not a bad mother, that every baby is different. She reassured me and gave me tips on how to handle my three-year-old and keep her involved with her new brother. It worked a treat but as my son was born such a big baby he was still feeding through the night. I contacted her again when my son was twenty-four weeks and explained his routine and she followed up with me on some very helpful tips and ideas and reassured me that it wasn't hunger – it was more likely to be a habit and that was why he was waking up. I followed her tips and within a week he was sleeping through the night, my toddler was sleeping on in the mornings and the whole family was feeling back to normal.

I just couldn't believe it. It was like someone had sent me an angel from heaven! I just couldn't believe this person who I contacted would help us out so much. She never pushed anything on me or made me feel like I was doing anything wrong. She made me feel like I was doing my best and that everything would fall into place and she was so right. I was blessed to have found and got in contact with her.

Niamh is a very kind and professional woman with a lot of love for her work and helping families. I hope any parent out there who needs some help or support will get in contact with her. She has helped my family so much.

P., Limerick

We got in touch with Niamh at The Nursery when our six-month-old was waking on the hour every hour and we were totally exhausted. We wondered how a consultation could change things but it certainly did! Niamh was perfectly professional but extremely understanding and non-judgmental. We loved her controlled 'comforting' rather than controlled crying approach as it meant that our baby never really got into an extreme state of distress and she knew that we were there to comfort her but had changed the goalposts a bit so that we, the grown-ups, were regaining control! Niamh showed a genuine interest in us by following up for the next week with calls or texts (with advice where needed) each morning. She was very approachable post-consultation, which was really valuable to us, and there was no extra cost for this service. All in all we would highly recommend Niamh – she made a huge improvement in our lives and indeed our little baby's. As she would say in her own words, the greatest gift that you can give to a child is sleep and the ability to settle themselves on their own. I would echo that sentiment but add that Niamh, by doing so, also gives a gift to the parents.

U., Dublin

We reached out to Niamh in order to get our toddler to be able to fall asleep on his own, in his bed and stay there for the night! As it stood, one of us was sharing a bed with him every night and god forbid we tried to have some time for ourselves. Our toddler ruled the roost when it came to bedtime and to be honest it was starting to really drain us both. We needed some expert advice which came in the form of Niamh. Godsend, lifesaver, whatever you want to call her, she gave us our life back. But most importantly our toddler is much happier and sleeping all night in his own bed.

K., Wicklow

When I encountered sleep issues with my second son, I did not hesitate in contacting Niamh as a highly regarded professional in this field.

I have found Niamh to be an exceptional and gifted individual. She encompasses a rare blend of qualities – Niamh is professional and dedicated, yet also warm, friendly and humorous. She is honest, reliable and enthusiastic.

A natural communicator, Niamh relates easily to parents and children alike. Kind, yet firm, Niamh's holistic approach to the entire family unit benefits all. Parents appreciate her encouragement and non-judgmental manner. Her simple and attainable methods have instant and lasting results, with no negative side effects.

Niamh is passionate about her work and achieving a favourable outcome for her clients. She is a pleasure to deal with and my family is testament to the success of her work.

A., Dublin

When my son was about four months old I was all over the place with his routine. As in, he didn't have one that made sense! My biggest issues were his naps and general afternoon activities. I contacted Niamh through a friend and she went through my whole day with me and made several suggestions such as shortening his early morning nap to get better value out of the lunchtime nap. This alone was a life-saver! I really couldn't see the woods for the trees and I was exhausted! Niamh was not only kind and really listened to me, but her advice was practical and made so much sense. Sometimes the advice from someone who has the knowledge but is not a family member is better received!! I never looked back and made contact several more times with Niamh about other issues with my son and she was always ready to listen and talk.

R., Meath

Niamh was an invaluable resource to us as first-time parents. In particular, she helped us get our daughter back into a good sleeping routine after we had gone through a rough patch of sleepless nights due to bad habits creeping in! We have not looked back since and will always be so grateful for all of the practical and really helpful tips that Niamh gave us. She really is 'Super-Niamhy'!

S., Dublin

APPENDIX 3

USEFUL CONTACT DETAILS

For further information on SIDS relevant to Ireland, contact:

National Sudden Infant Death Register/SIDS Ireland
Children's University Hospital
Temple Street
Dublin 1
Phone: 01 8788455
Free phone: 1800 332 332
Email: npmr@cuh.ie
Web: www.sidsireland.ie

The Irish Sudden Infant Death Association
Carmichael House
4 North Brunswick Street
Dublin 7
Phone: 1850 391 391

For guidelines on safe sleeping:

National Institute for Health and Care Excellence (NICE)
10 Spring Gardens

London
SW1A 2BU
England
Phone: +44(0)300 323 0140
Email: nice@nice.org.uk
Web: www.nice.org.uk

For breastfeeding support:
www.breastfeeding.ie
www.kellymom.com

For information on Sleepytot Bunny:
www.sleepytot.com

www.HerFamily.ie – a practical, positive parenting website